The Teachers Practical Stress and Workload Survival Guide

The Teachers Practical Stress and Workload Survival Guide

Mike Culley C.Psychol. AFBPsS
www.teacherwellbeing.uk

First Edition 2023

To Jane

A wonderful teacher who always goes the extra mile...

Contents

Some Notes on Terminology

This book is designed to be helpful for everyone working in education. Whether you are a teacher, lecturer, support staff or administrator, and you work with 'children', 'pupils' or 'students', in a school, college, university or other educational facility, there is something here for you.

However, whilst the applicability is far wider, to keep things concise and readable, I have used the single terms 'teacher', 'pupil' and 'school' throughout...

Free Wellbeing Resources

You can find more resources, including audio guides, suggestions for further reading, and much more at my website www.teacherwellbeing.uk

How to Use this Book

Many books that have a structure with different sections suggest that you can dip in and out of them randomly. However, to get the most out of this book, it will be most effective to first read it right through in order to build up an understanding of stress and workload, as well as some of the possible solutions. Doing so will provide an important opportunity to reflect on those aspects to which you may be able to most effectively make changes to reduce your stress levels, and help you to deal with workload.

Then, armed with this knowledge, revisiting those particular sections which have the ideas that you want to apply, and reviewing the relevant ideas and techniques, will pay dividends.

However, if you do wish to get to the most important practical sections more quickly, and perhaps already have good understanding of stress and the way it works, then skip to start reading at the section on personality (part 2), and go on from there.

All of the ideas herein are effective, and are used by many teachers, but please do be aware that not everything works for everybody. Human beings are wonderfully varied, and while many techniques contained within will be right for you, there will be others that won't, due to circumstances, personality and/or preference.

You may also find that tweaking these techniques may sometimes make them suit you better. That's fine – these are helpful and effective ideas that you might use, rather than unbendable rules about how things must be done. As everyone is an individual, selecting the right techniques and, where necessary, altering them to work optimally for you, is the best approach.

The most important thing is to step back and consider the possibilities of what might work for you, and then to actually make those changes that you need to make.

The Spidergraph.

In order to overcome stress, and get on top of workload, it's important to understand exactly where you might do things differently in order to have the greatest impact on your wellbeing.

This is where you can use a spidergraph as a reflection tool. A copy of the spidergraph for this book is in the appendix at the end of it, or it can be downloaded from my website and printed off for you to use. Go to **www.teacherwellbeing.uk** to download a copy.

I would strongly recommend that you do this exercise. Talking to many teachers, both on workshops and when working one-one, they have often found that the insights provided by the spidergraph have created a useful starting point for reflection, and for deciding where to make changes.

Take a few moments now to look at the spidergraph in the appendix, or download your own copy, and read about how to use it. Then, return here and we can begin our journey into dealing with stress and workload…

Introduction

Being a teacher can be one of the most important and rewarding occupations.

Of course, if you are an teacher, you will know that, but you will also be very aware that the teaching profession is not quite the occupation that many people outside schools believe it to be.

Many outsiders, unaware of the realities of school life, view it as an easy role, where teachers finish early each day by 3.30pm, and have those long relaxing summer breaks lasting a whole six weeks, in addition to plentiful other holidays…

A lovely, easy profession?…

As a teacher you know the reality that, whilst incredibly rewarding, it can also be one of the most stressful and challenging of occupations.

Today, issues of stress and burnout mean that far too many excellent and experienced teachers are leaving the profession. This creates a situation that isn't good for the pupils, their schools, or the teachers themselves. But it doesn't have to be this way as there are tools, techniques, and approaches that provide powerful and practical ways to help to develop a resilient mindset, deal with high levels of workload, and overcome stress.

Over the past few years, working with many individual teachers and schools, as well as local authorities and teaching unions, I've brought together a range of different ideas to help teachers explore practical solutions to problems of stress, workload and burnout.

Of course, it could be easy to come up with ideas which aren't realistic to apply in the real world. However, this book contains only those ideas that are based on many years of successful one-one and group work with teachers and schools. They are solutions that work in the real world for many different individuals in a range of settings.

I have to sincerely thank the many teachers who, over the past few years, have generously shared their own approaches and techniques for staying on top of workload and stress.

Every idea you will find here is used by many teachers on a daily basis. Of course individual situations vary greatly, so there will be some ideas here that are not applicable for you, or tools that are not practical to use at this time. That's ok, because there will also be others that you can use successfully.

I would suggest that you think of this book rather as a buffet of ideas – something to explore and take away those techniques that will work best for you. Within, you'll find ideas ranging from the obvious (but included as they are often forgotten or ignored) to the subtle and even the counter-intuitive.

Here I should add a word of warning. It is very easy to look for a quick and easy solution that will solve all of your stress and workload problems in one go. However, as your school is probably not Hogwarts, there's no magic wand available to cast a spell that will instantly make all the problems go away. The ideas you will find within are tried and trusted, and they do work, but while many can have quite a rapid impact, others need to be applied effectively and consistently over some time.

Also, beware that it can be very easy to fall into the mindset of thinking that nothing is going to work for you, or believing that while something may be a good idea for others, for whatever reason you couldn't use it yourself. If you find yourself saying that to yourself, please do step back and do challenge yourself as to whether that is really the case...

It is also important to carefully consider where you could make the most effective changes for you, so do use the spidergraph - many teachers have commented to me about how useful they have found this.

It is often said that all change comes from within. This book can give you ideas, but cannot actually change how you feel, reduce your stress, and help you stay on top of workload unless you actually use some of the ideas within to make changes to what you do, and how you do it.

Remember the famous quote attributed to Einstein, which was his definition of insanity - "doing the same thing over and over again and expecting different results...". If you want to feel different you've got to do something different!

"Insanity – doing the same thing over and over again and expecting different results"

Another reason for some teachers resisting doing things differently is the belief that this means getting less done. In fact, it certainly doesn't, as if we are tired, stressed and exhausted we actually become increasingly unproductive and error-prone. By dealing with the stresses that we face we can get far more done in less time, and make less mistakes.

How many times have you been exhausted and set out to do some work, and realised that you have spent hours working, yet achieving little of worth? By reducing stress and building inner energy and focus you can be more productive, with the bonus of giving you more time for other important things.

I will also occasionally comment through the book based upon my own experience, and personal thoughts. Many years ago, it was experiencing work related stress and anxiety myself that led me to explore solutions through applied psychology and other techniques, and started me on the path to where I am today. I will share some of my own ideas on these techniques and approaches as we go through the book ...

Many teachers today live in the hope that their incredible work ethic, and going the extra mile for their pupils, will be noticed by their schools senior leadership, who will thereby highly value their work and realise the intense pressures they are under. Doing so, they hope that senior leaders will then change things to reduce that workload. Maybe that does happen in some schools, but overall the signs aren't good, so it's sensible to take control of your own well-being.

Finally, in my work I've had fascinating discussions with some teaching union officials who feel that it's shouldn't be up to individual teachers to adapt to the situation. Instead, their schools should change their culture and become supportive workplaces where stress and workload isn't an issue. Absolutely, I agree! In many places, school culture does need to change, and perhaps one day it may even happen...

However, right now I don't see nearly enough movement in this direction. There's a lot of rhetoric and discussion, and some forward thinking schools are making some really positive changes, but it's not universal and it's not happening fast or far enough.

The wellbeing and workload crisis for teachers is here and now, and so whilst striving for a more supportive environment nationally, I believe it's important for teachers to try and find more immediate personal solutions to support their own resilience, positively engage with their teaching roles, and once again enjoy making an important difference for their pupils.

So, let's begin…

Part 1 - Understanding Stress

Dealing with stress is important. Chronic stress can lead to serious psychological and medical issues, as the physical and mental strain that stress puts on the individual is considerable.

A good way to begin your journey to greater resilience is by understanding the way in which stress actually works, as well as knowing some of the many signs of stress to look out for.

However, do be aware that some of the symptoms of stress are the same as symptoms of other physical illness. It's vital to first ensure that the symptoms you are suffering are due to situational stress and not to anything else that should be addressed medically.

1.1 - How Does Stress Work?

One of the best known models of stress is the 'fight or flight' syndrome. According to this, human beings, in common with many animals, evolved important physical and mental reactions as a way to deal with threatening situations that they faced.

Imagine if, millennia ago, you were suddenly confronted with a real and immediate threat such as a dangerous wild animal, or enemy tribesman. In this situation you could either fight it, or run away from it – fight or flight. (There is actually a third response, which is to freeze - the idea being that by doing so it makes us less visible. Human beings do sometimes freeze in threatening situations. However, fighting or fleeing is more common, and when we freeze the physiological response is the same.)

Now, whether you are getting ready to fight or flee, your body needs to prepare, and both options utilise a very similar internal physical response.

The Fight or Flight response is common to animals and human beings.

For instance adrenaline is released around the body in order to prime it for action. Meanwhile, our breathing rate changes as we need to pump our muscles full of oxygen to work efficiently, and our heart rate increases to increase the blood flow and move fuel for energy around the body.

Because our external muscles need that oxygen in order to work effectively, the blood flow tends to move away from the internal organs of the body, such as your digestive system, and towards the muscles of the limbs where it's most needed - after all if you are trying to avoid being something else's next meal, you don't need to spend energy digesting your own previous one! This, of course, is one of the reasons why we tend to get a dodgy tummy when we are anxious...

There are also cognitive shifts as well, because to survive we need to focus almost exclusively on the threat - after all if you are faced with a wild animal slowly stalking you as its potential prey, taking time out to examine the wild flowers that surround you isn't going to be a productive use of your attention. It makes sense to stay completely focused on whatever the threat may be.

These responses work, and are highly appropriate and effective for the survival situations that they evolved for. Crucially, all these physical and cognitive responses are designed to be a short term response, lasting only a few minutes until the situation is resolved. As such it's very effective in priming us for the action that we may well need to take to survive.

In the modern world, this ancient response has two important aspects that make it more problematic. Firstly, the subconscious mind doesn't really know the difference between various types of threats, and secondly, the fact that it was designed to be a very short term response...

The intense physical effects of the flight or fight response are fine for a few minutes, after which we should ideally return to a calmer, more relaxed mode, switching off this heightened alert state. However, today we have many different perceived threats, such as deadlines, angry parents, lesson observations, and red gas bills, and our subconscious often reacts to these in exactly the same way as it would to a tiger creeping up on us in the undergrowth – as a perceived threat triggering fight or flight...

It may seem excessive for our system to respond in this intense way to modern, non-lethal threats. However, our subconscious tends to treat threats in similar ways…

Naturally, these modern perceived threats don't resolve in only a few minutes, leaving us in this intense threat state for an extended period, or even constantly. This is where stress can become harmful, as this has physical as well as psychological impacts on wellbeing.

The fight or flight model also explains why we constantly think and worry about the problems that we are facing — often making things seem worse. Just as you would focus exclusively upon a wild creature stalking you, you keep your mental focus upon whatever the problem is — it goes round and round in your mind as your subconscious keeps trying to find a resolution or escape from it. Unfortunately, solutions are not so easy to find for modern stressors…

1.2 - The Signs of Stress

So what are some of the signs of stress to look out for? There are a range of symptoms, such as…

- Frequent Headaches
- Upset Stomach (which can include diarrhoea, constipation and/or nausea)
- Aches, Pains, and Tense Muscles
- Chest Pain
- Rapid Heartbeat
- Insomnia
- Low energy

- Frequent Colds and Infections
- Loss of Sexual Desire and/or Ability
- Nervousness and Shaking
- Ringing in the Ears
- Excess Sweating
- Dry Mouth
- Clenched Jaw
- Grinding Teeth

Whenever I'm running a teachers resilience workshop, I can often see people quietly doing a mental checklist, and some (actually, often a large number) then start to look concerned when they realise just how many symptoms they may be already experiencing without having realised it!

Are you experiencing stress symptoms?

Take a few moments to think about just how many of these you personally might be currently experiencing. It's important to be aware of this, because one of the one of the challenges is that stress will often slowly and insidiously creep up on us. It can increase quite gradually, so we tend not to notice just how stressed we're becoming until it becomes overwhelming.

Another issue is that many people may begin to realise that they are under pressure, and that their stress levels are building up, but tell themselves that it's only temporary and so they don't need to do anything about it. For example, a teacher may be aware that they have taken on extra workload, and the pressures that this brings, but tell themselves that it will only be until the end of term. But, of course, by the time the end of term comes, something else will have taken its place and the stress continues...

Burnout

There are many different definitions of stress, and also many definitions of burnout. Burnout can be caused by doing too much for too long, leading to physical exhaustion, or suffering stress for an extended period leading to psychological exhaustion (or both).

One useful way to think of burnout and differentiate it from stress is that when we are under stress, we are using up our inner psychological capital – rather like a phone battery running down. We are functioning, but we are using up more of our inner physical and/or psychological energy stores than we are replacing...

If we are not careful we can run out entirely – that is burnout. Burnout is where there's nothing left – our inner psychological and physical resources are spent, and rather like our mobile phone without any battery power, when we reach that point doing anything becomes almost impossible.

Now many of the signs of burnout are very similar to the signs of stress in many ways. But despite this overlap, there are some additional symptoms which can make burnout even more challenging for teachers…

So what are the signs of burnout to look out for? They include…

- Impaired Concentration
- Chronic Fatigue
- Impaired Immunity
- Forgetfulness
- Depression
- Anger
- Anxiety
- Low Appetite
- Low Motivation
- Cynicism/Pessimism
- Detachment/Isolation

Now, I'm assuming that you may have once again undertaken a little personal checklist as you read down the list – how did you do?

These symptoms all demonstrate the potential effects of burnout upon our health and well-being. However, they can also impact a teaching role in another direct way.

As you see from the list, burnout can lead to cynicism and pessimism, as well as detachment and isolation. This is why, if a teacher is suffering from burnout, it can change their attitude about teaching from the excitement they felt as a newly qualified teacher (or early career teachers they are today) to an attitude of cynicism and pessimism. They may begin to feel detached from their colleagues around them leaving them feeling increasingly negative and isolated. From here, it is a short path to leaving the profession…

However, it's not all gloom! Over many years of working with people, I have found that individuals have a great capacity to recover. The mind and body is a system that can be effectively self-balancing and self-healing, and given the chance it will return to a healthy and comfortable state – provided it hasn't been pushed too far, which then requires a much longer recovery. To achieve this, however, it means really finding ways to create the space, conditions, and techniques to help this recovery and build resilience.

Ensure you safeguard your resilience…

Provided a person hasn't been pushed far as burnout, they can begin to bounce back reasonably quickly.

If a person has burned out, however, it does take longer to recover – often considerably longer. Be aware that if you are already suffering burnout it can be very easy to assume that when you start to feel better, everything is now fine and you are back to the old you.

However, thinking this is almost certainly a mistake, and acting on it can be disastrous. In my experience of working with those having reached the burnout stage, it actually takes an extended time to fully recover and rebuild inner resilience. Until that point is achieved the recovery is far more fragile than it appears and the individual is still extremely vulnerable to renewed stressors. If you overdo things too quickly, before the inner strength has really returned, you can easily be overwhelmed once more.

So, if you are suffering burnout, it is vital to take the time to rebuild your resilience properly, and to make sure that you are strong enough before you take everything on once more.

So, stress and burnout are an important issue to be aware of. Could it be particularly acute or likely for teachers? Let's explore that next....

Part 2 - The Personality of Teachers.

Some years ago, while the graduate teacher programme was a popular entry route into teaching, I did considerable work with a teacher training provider supporting the selection and initial training of teachers. During this, I undertook psychometrics of both teachers and would-be teachers to understand their personalities, and so to support the trainees through the challenging training program.

Examining the results, I found that the personality profile of a teacher appeared to be interesting, and quite different to the majority of the population. Now, be aware that we were focusing on understanding and supporting individuals, so I didn't undertake an in-depth statistical analysis of the overall group to confirm this beyond statistical doubt, but there did appear to be a very marked trend in terms of the personality of our teachers and would-be teachers in three key aspects.

Firstly it was obvious that many (or most) teachers personality tended towards the highly perfectionist. Secondly, they were extremely rule conscious, and thirdly they were optimistic and positive about human nature - they saw the best in people

So, the personality profile could suggest that we have a group of people who tend to have very high standards, leading to a desire to do an outstanding job, who see the best in their pupils and believe in them and their abilities to grow and succeed, and also who follow the rules.

Is that the profile that we'd want for a teacher? I think it is - if I was sending my child to a school that's exactly how I would want the teachers there to be. So, many teachers personality steers them towards dedication and excellence. That's fantastic in terms of professionalism and doing a great job.

Teachers — Perfectionist, and Positive...

However what makes an outstanding teacher can potentially also generate a vulnerability in terms of stress levels. The perfectionism that drives a teacher to create outstanding lessons, can also increase stress by their constantly trying to do too much.

The positive view of human nature means that teachers believe in the potential of their pupils, but also can be taken advantage of. Finally the desire to follow the rules means that a teacher may create a structured classroom, but also want to follow each and every rule - including those unwritten ones that are part of the way a school runs, such as the expectation of needing to put in extra hours each and every day, and not leaving on time...

Understanding this and using this personality positively is something which we will discuss more later on, but for now it's important to remember that some of the inner stresses may emerge from an innate desire for excellence of many teachers...

If teachers personality and drive to be outstanding for their pupils makes them more likely to suffer stress, what are the techniques that can help overcome it?...

Part 3 – Some Effective De-Stressing Techniques

Naturally, if you are suffering from stress, the first thing that you want to do is to reduce it quickly, so in this section we turn to some effective ways for reducing levels of stress and tension.

To begin to de-stress, you need ways to switch off the fight or flight response, and create a sense of calmness and wellbeing. There are many different methods to achieve this, and which are going to be most effective for you is very individual - an approach that works well for one person really won't work nearly as well for another. Therefore I would suggest trying different ideas to see which ones will be the best fit for you.

We will start this journey by exploring some of the many traditional approaches to de-stressing, including breathing exercises, meditation, mindfulness, and other similar techniques. These exercises and techniques have been around for a long time for the simple reason that they can work really well.

However, although powerful, they take practice and persistence. Be aware that psychological fitness is, in many ways, similar to physical fitness - just as people don't go to the gym once and then expect to be super fit, it also takes time and commitment to reduce stresses and build resilience. When it comes to psychological fitness and wellbeing, a regime of repeated regular relaxation exercises can have the same effect on the anxious and stressed mind as regular exercise does for the physically unfit body.

The exercises and ideas in this section can be mixed and matched to suit you. For example, meditation and breathing exercises usually go well together, or you might do a progressive relaxation, while using breathing exercises and also listening to relaxing music. Experiment and see what seems best for you...

Find the right combination of techniques to suit you...

As with any technique do be aware that no approach works for everybody, and a very few individuals may react in an unexpected way. For example, there are some people for whom doing breathing exercises can actually increase their anxiety – it's rare but it can occur. If you find that this is the case for you with a given technique, then just stop, and explore something different.

3.1 - Breathing Exercises.

We start with one of the most popular and classic destressing approaches – breathing exercises.

You may already have encountered breathing exercises in other contexts such as doing yoga etc. They can be very powerful at helping to achieve a relaxed state, as when we enter the fight or flight state our breathing rate changes quite considerably by going into a panic response mode. This usually involves more rapid breathing from higher in the chest.

However, when we are relaxed, we tend to breathe from lower down, and breathe more slowly using the diaphragm. By adopting a more relaxed breathing mode we can persuade our subconscious mind that we are actually relaxed, and that can then help to calm our whole system.

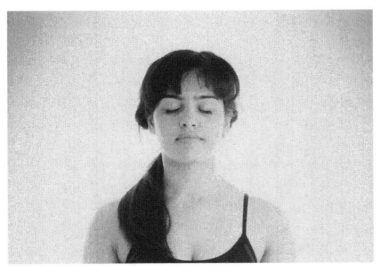

Breathing exercises can be powerful de-stressors

Some people find that, if they haven't been breathing effectively for some time, at first they can feel lightheaded when changing to a deeper and more efficient breathing pattern. If this is the case for you, return to your old breathing pattern for a while and the feeling will pass. Usually, you get more used to the breathing exercise with practice, and this lightheaded feeling stops occurring, but take it carefully.

One of the useful things about breathing exercises is that they can be pretty much done anywhere and at any time, and can also form a valuable adjunct to some of the other relaxation exercises we're going to be discussing shortly.

If you're stuck in a traffic jam rather than getting frustrated, why not just stop and do a breathing exercise (eyes open!), and it can help you stay calm and relaxed. It can even be done while you're watching television (although if you're watching EastEnders perhaps that's more likely to get you stressed and frustrated than relaxed!).

Also, other people won't necessarily realise you're doing a breathing exercise as it can be done quite subtly, so you can just sit there in the evening (or in a meeting…) and do some relaxation without anybody knowing.

What to Do – A Breathing Exercise
Note: A free downloadable audio guide for this exercise can be found at www.teacherwellbeing.uk

The exercise I'm going to suggest is quite straightforward. It consists of a few different elements, but if some of the aspects of the exercise don't work for you then do feel free to change them.

You may find it more powerful to close your eyes during this exercise, but this isn't vital.

Now to start with, I'd like you to become aware of how you are currently breathing. You can do this by placing one hand on your chest and the other on your belly. Noticing which of the two hands is moving most can suggest whether you are breathing from high in the chest, or using your diaphragm and so lower belly breathing.

How do you breathe?

Now for the breathing exercise itself. The first element is to breathe in through your nose, and then out through your mouth. This is a classic part of many breathing exercises and certainly helps, but if it isn't comfortable or doesn't feel right for you that's not a problem - simply breathe in whatever way feels better.

Secondly, slow your breathing down, and try to make each breath as smooth as you can. Don't over breathe, but do breathe fully.

Remember that when we're in the fight or flight mode our breathing tends to shift to the chest and away from the relaxed mode belly breathing. We need to change this, so if necessary, try to shift your breathing from chest breathing down to belly breathing. Get your diaphragm working try to make the breaths come from low down in your torso…

Now comes a really important part of the exercise which is to notice how long it takes you to breathe in by a silent count in your mind. You might perhaps find that you inhale for a count of four, but however many your inbreath count is for, is fine. Now breathe out, and try to take at least twice as long to breathe out as you did to breathe in. So if you inhaled for a count of four, then try and exhale for a count of eight. If you can't quite make it to eight that's OK, as it's one of those things that can improve with practise.

It's the extended exhalation that is actually central to making this exercise as relaxing as possible. One possible reason for this is that when we breathe in, our heart rate increases - breathing in is energising – and when we exhale our heart rate actually decreases and we relax. By breathing in and then breathing out for at least twice as long, your mind feels an energising in-breath but then the far longer exhalation which is more relaxing overall.

Continue this for the rest of the time you are doing the exercise for…

So how long is long enough for this exercise? The answer is, ideally, for as long as possible! But looking at it more practically, I have found that, where practical, 15 to 20 minutes can make quite a profound difference to how you feel.

It often takes at least 10 or 15 minutes for the fight or flight response to begin switch off, and at this point, many people make the mistake of stopping the breathing exercise because they think they've achieved the relaxation they were seeking. However, when you achieve and then maintain this relaxed state, it gives your mind (and body) time to recharge, recover, and recentre. So the longer you can stay in this relaxed state the better it is for you.

What to Do – Some Breathing Exercise Variations

Now there are many variations on breathing exercises that you might like to try - indeed, there are entire books just containing a wide range of them. Here are a few variations you might experiment with…

One is the 4,4,4 breathing pattern. In this, you breathe in for a count of 4, hold it for 4, and then exhale for 4 before repeating.

Another variant is the 4, 4, 6, 2 version. This is where you breathe in for a count of 4, hold that breath for 4, exhale over a count of 6, and then hold for a count of 2 before repeating. This one is used in some yoga practices.

Some Personal Thoughts

Breathing exercises are something which I myself use and I find them really effective. Whenever I'm working with people it's one of the first techniques I suggest because they are so straightforward, and can be applied almost anywhere and at any time.

However, perhaps because they are so straightforward and almost obvious, people often forget to do them or feel that they won't make a difference. It's important, therefore, to stick at it and give breathing exercises a chance to work...

3.2 - Progressive Relaxation.

Progressive relaxation can be a very effective technique for achieving deep relaxation. It is a gentle but powerful exercise, that is worth taking some time to do well. Like any technique its effectiveness improves with practice, and the effects tend to be cumulative so the results will increase over time with repeated sessions. It has the advantage that it is quite straightforward and can really help to release the physical tensions of stress.

By deeply and gradually relaxing the body, you feel less physical tension which helps to break the stress feedback loop.

What to Do – Progressive Relaxation
Note: A free downloadable audio guide to this exercise can be found at www.teacherwellbeing.uk

Start by finding somewhere that you can really relax, and won't be disturbed – relaxing on a sofa or bed is fine.

The basics of the technique are really quite simple. Just start with one part of the body and relax it as deeply as you can.

Then move on to the next part, relax that, and so on, working your way through your whole body.

The exercise is pretty flexible - where you start your relaxation is up to you. You might start with your feet and work your way up your body from there, or you might start with your chest and work out to the different parts of your body. Some people like to tense the muscles in each part before relaxing it, as the contrast of tense-relaxed makes the relaxation feel more profound.

Although simple, there are a couple of important things to bear in mind with progressive relaxation to make it most effective. One is to take it slowly, and really focus on as small a part of the body as possible for a reasonable amount of time before moving on. For instance, rather than relaxing your whole arm at once, start off by relaxing each finger one at a time, then relax the palms of your hands, followed by your wrists and so on, working your slowly up your arm and taking enough time at each point to really allow it to relax.

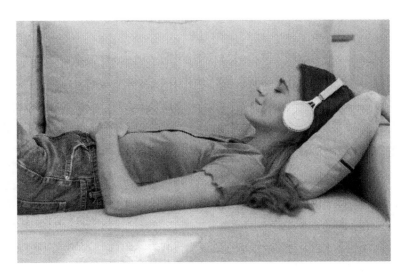

Find somewhere comfortable to relax.

If you're also doing a breathing exercise (and breathing exercises can work nicely with progressive relaxation) you might tie in each step of relaxation with your breathing. So, you breathe in and as you slowly exhale you relax one finger. Then you breathe in once more, and as you exhale, relax the next finger, and so on. This can helps keep things nice and slow and combines the breathing with the progressive relaxation in a natural way.

Once you've worked your way around the whole of your body once, it can be good to go back and go around your body again, this time changing your focus to be on relaxing larger parts, in order to relax them even more deeply.

You might also scan through your body to find any parts which are perhaps still less relaxed. Some areas of your body may need you to focus on them for longer - the shoulders for instance quite often seem to maintain that bit of tension.

3.3 – Music for Relaxation

The right music can make a wonderful aid to relaxation.

Many people find listening to music relaxing. This relaxing effect is supported by studies that show that music does positively change our response to stress. Therefore, adding some suitable music to your relaxation routine can make sense...

What to Do – Using Music for Relaxation

Probably the most effective way to use music is as a part of a larger relaxation regime. One approach that I recommend is to combine a breathing exercise with listening to some music – about 20 minutes or so of listening to the right music whilst undertaking a breathing exercise can create a powerfully relaxing experience. Why not add in some progressive relaxation too?..

In terms of what music to listen to, naturally it's very much down to personal choice. However, do remember that music can have very powerful connections to our thoughts, and so trigger emotions based on past memories and experiences. You may have experienced the 'our song' syndrome where hearing a particular tune or song reminds you of a particular time, place or situation, and the linked feelings come flooding back which might be exciting, romantic, happy, or sad.

Listening to music can help you relax...

For effective relaxation, ideally you really want something which is unconnected with any earlier feelings, so that when you listen to it can simply relax.

Also, by using music you don't hear elsewhere, you begin to make new associations for that music with the state of deep relaxation - if you do this often enough what you will find is that, after a while, just putting on the music helps to trigger the relaxation you seek.

I would also suggest that, generally, instrumental music can be better than songs with lyrics. Perhaps try some new age music, as many people find that this works well for them. Much of this can be really relaxing and is usually lyric free.

Some Personal Thoughts

One of my own favourites when I'm relaxing is early Mike Oldfield such as Tubular Bells, Ommadawn and Hergest Ridge. I find these work really well for me, and have the added benefits that they were created in the days of the traditional LP record. This means each track is one side of a vinyl album, and therefore about 20 minutes in length, so when I listen to it I have a natural timer to an approximately 20 minute relaxation period.

Therefore, I don't have to think about how long I've been relaxing or need set an external timer, as one side of the original album is the right duration for a pleasant relaxation…

Another personal favourite is a selection of new age music – especially some early works by Tim Wheater, whose 'A Calmer Panorama' combines atmospheric sound effects with flute.

3.4 – Meditation and Similar Techniques

Now, lets begin to explore some classic mind-based relaxation techniques…

There are many and varied schools of meditation, which involve a range of differing approaches and practices. Space means that we can only really take a look at one or two of them here, but I hope that if you try the following, and find it useful, you may wish to explore other possibilities further.

A popular view of meditation is that it often involves clearing the mind entirely of any thought whatsoever – to turn the mind into a blank slate. Now I'm not sure if it's just the western mind, but most people seem to have great difficulty in actually doing this, or even getting anywhere close to it! In all my time working with people I've only encountered two individuals who were able to just stop their thoughts entirely (and I'm still not sure exactly how they did it…).

However, meditation isn't that prescriptive, and more often actually involves focus, rather than blankness...

As with many of the approaches we discuss, the effects of meditation techniques are cumulative, and build over time. Regular practice can really make a difference.

What to Do – A Simple Meditation Exercise

First find somewhere quiet that you won't be disturbed. Sit in a comfortable position – it doesn't need to be the traditional yoga pose…

Now, close your eyes and focus upon your breathing. As you inhale, think the works 'breathing in' and as you exhale, 'breathing out'.

Continue this practice for increasing periods of time, starting with using this meditation for only a few minutes a day, and slowly building up until you reach 20 minutes or so.

When thinking about timing this exercise, it can be tempting to keep opening your eyes and seeing if the time is up yet... Naturally, this is not conducive to focus and relaxation! Instead, set a timer for the amount of time that you wish to meditate for, and then do the meditation until the alarm goes.

Meditation can be effective, and you don't need to do the pose!...

As you meditate, especially at first, random thoughts will pop into your mind. If so, acknowledge them, and then try to let them go by gently returning your focus to your breathing and the phrases.

Of course many people do find this initially rather challenging, but adherents of meditation do find that there are many powerful benefits of developing an ability to meditate effectively.

Within meditation, a mantra is an word, sound or phrase which is repeated over and over again, and this focussed breathing technique focuses your thoughts upon a neutral 'mantra' (the 'breathing in' and 'breathing out'). However, there are many different mantras that you might try.

You might experiment with words in English, such as 'Peace', or 'Calm'. From traditional meditation practice, probably the most well-known mantra is 'om mani padme hum' (you will often find variations of the spelling) which some translate as "praise to the jewel in the lotus".

Give it a try, and see if it works for you.

3.5 - Mindfulness

A modern meditation practise that has aspects in common with traditional meditation, but also some alternative elements, is mindfulness. Mindfulness has become incredibly popular over the last few years, being recommended for stress, anxiety, and other similar psychological challenges. It involves being focused in the moment – in the here and now.

Mindfulness differs from clearing your mind or focusing on a mantra by being focused instead on the experience of being here and now. This awareness is ideally non-judgmental and non-evaluative, so you just notice what's happening rather than necessarily have a thought or opinion about it.

So you might be sitting there, undertaking the mindfulness body scan exercise (which follows), and notice that there are some sounds coming from outside the room. So, instead of feeling frustration at this, you aim to just notice the sounds, and avoid thinking about them being good or bad.

If you get an itch in your leg you just notice that there is an itch in your leg, but you don't think about it as annoying. Instead it is just something that is happening.

What to Do - Mindfulness (Using A Body Scan Meditation).

Note: A free downloadable audio guide to this exercise can be found at www.teacherwellbeing.uk

Mindfulness has many varied practices, so here is a simple one to start with, which also highlights some differences to 'traditional' meditation.

Start by finding a relaxing and comfortable position. It might be sitting or lying down. Now, become aware of your breath. Breathe slowly and deeply (but don't overdo it). Focus on your inhalation and exhalation, and the feeling of movement of the air in and out of your body.

Now, select a part of the body and notice any sensations there. It may be tension, or relaxation, it may be an itch or discomfort! Just focus and notice any sensations there, as you continue to breathe slowly and deeply.

Take you time to really become aware of the sensations in each part of your body, before moving on to the next. Remember that this exercise involves acknowledging the sensations in your body, not judging them. Any emotions triggered by these sensations can also be noted, but accepted.

Continue this right round your whole body.

As you do this your thoughts may wander. That's not a problem, simply bring them back gently to the focus of the current awareness.

Continue this exercise for 20 minutes to gain the full benefit.

As with many relaxation and meditation techniques, you may wish to build slowly up to the 20 minutes daily if you have never tried any form of meditation before, or are rusty. Also, remember that the benefits themselves are gradual and cumulative, but worthwhile.

3.6 - The Imaginary Journey.

Much of meditation is about quieting the mind through focus. However, the idea of the imaginary journey is instead to create a mini break in the mind. It is actually subtler technique than it may, at first, appear.

You may be well aware that it's very difficult to not think about stress and anxiety, to push away the worries and concerns that play on our mind. It is like the idea of telling someone not to think of the colour blue - the more they try not to think it, the more they have to think of it in order not to! Similarly, trying not to think of your worries and concerns means you have to be continually aware of them, which isn't helpful.

Instead of trying to push away out worries and concerns therefore, it can be powerful to simply replace them with more pleasant thoughts. To do this we utilise what is known as Miller's magic number. George Miller was a cognitive psychologist who investigated the capacity of our short term memory - that is how many things we can hold in our short-term memory at any one time. His experiments suggested that for most people it's around 7, plus or minus 2, items, and thus we can hold between 5 and 9 things in our mind at any one time with an average of 7 (this is why mobile phone numbers are hard to remember – there are too many digits for most peoples short term memory capacity).

We can only keep between 5 and 9 things in our working memory…

Applying this to our imaginary journey, if you can keep seven or so elements of that scene in your mind at once, there is no room left for your worries and concerns. Instead of trying not to think about them, you are simply filling your mind with more pleasant and relaxing thoughts and therefore giving it a break from worry to centre and relax. The key, of course, is to think of these seven or so things simultaneously, as least as much as possible...

So let's imagine that our relaxing place is a beach as an example, it might involve thinking about the colour of the sea, and simultaneously trying to notice the blue colour of the sky, and see the shape of the clouds drifting across it. Doing it at the same time, as much as possible, rather than switching from one to the next, is important. Yes, this is a little bit of mental gymnastics, but the more you can do to keep multiple elements in your mind, the better.

Again this takes a little bit of practise but if you become good at it you'll find that at the end of a imaginary journey you really can feel quite wonderfully relaxed.

What to Do - The Imaginary Journey.
Note: A free downloadable audio guide to this exercise can be found at www.teacherwellbeing.uk

As part of the exercise, we will imagine a relaxing scene, and use our senses to engage with different aspects of it. Making it realistic through using the senses is an important contributor to its effectiveness.

The first part is quite straightforward, and that is to select somewhere that, for you, is a relaxing or destressing place. Somewhere which takes you away from your current worries and concerns. Naturally, for most people this is somewhere like a beautiful tranquil beach, or sitting by a babbling brook enjoying the scenery, but it really is very much whatever works for you.

Remember as it is in your imagination, it can be somewhere you've been, or somewhere that you would like to go, or even some fantastic location purely from your imagination.

To start this exercise just close your eyes and try and visualise what you'd see if you were there, seeing it from the first person if you can - that is, as if looking through your own eyes.

Something to be aware of here is that people have different levels of ability to imagine images in their minds eye. Some people can create incredibly detailed images, whilst others really struggle to get a clear picture in their mind at all. So just do your best with it, and don't worry too much if you can't get a clear picture - just get what you can.

Finding your relaxing place…

Now, in your imagination, start to look around and become aware of the different details in the scene. See all of the different shapes and colours and textures. Notice little details – for example if you're on a beach you might see the colour of the ocean, and the colour of the sky, and you might notice the shape of the clouds, or the grains of sand on the beach. You might notice seashells and so on. Become aware of many different facets of what you're seeing in your mind's eye as if you were there, as that immersion is a really crucial element of a successful visualisation.

Now having explored the visual sense it's time to move on to the auditory sense, your hearing, and explore what sounds might be heard within your scene. Once again, imagine as many different aspects as you can.

So if we once again imagine that we are on the beach, then we might hear the sound of the waves, and hear any sea birds, and perhaps even notice the sound of a warm breeze blowing past us. Maybe there are other sonic aspects of the scene you might hear in your mind, so try and bring in as many as you can.

Next it's about introducing the sense of touch, so imagine any sensations of touch or feeling within the scene.

On our beach you might imagine feeling the sand between your toes, and the warmth of the sun on your skin, or the feeling of that warm breeze blowing past you. You might experience paddling in the ocean and feeling the cool of the water contrasting with the heat of the sun, and feeling the way the water flows past you as the waves flow in and out. Imagining the use of this sense of touch could be a really powerful way of taking yourself deeper into that scene.

As you might imagine, having explored sight sound and touch, if there are any aspects of smell or taste in scene that you can imagine that's a wonderful aspect to bring in.

This is often a very challenging aspect that many find really difficult, so if you can't get anything here don't worry. However, scent is actually a very evocative element of memory and forms quite a powerful aspect of many places, for example on our beach remembering the smell of the sea.

Now you have created this place in your mind, spend some time in your scene, as long as you can maintaining that focus on the varied aspects of your senses, and notice how relaxed you feel at the end.

Use as many senses as you can...

To develop it further, you might imagine moving through the scene, perhaps interacting with it in some way, such as a walk along the beach gradually discovering new details, or paddling in the ocean…

Some Personal Thoughts

I enjoy this exercise, and have found that many people also really love it. An important key to success is that the place in your mind really is somewhere that is relaxing for you.

Sometimes my clients feel that it has to be somewhere stereotypically relaxing, like the tropical beach, but this really isn't the case.

For one client, her relaxing place was a somewhat boisterous and noisy bar in South America! It really doesn't matter, its simply somewhere that will take you away from your pressures and stresses.

⬟ Reflection – Spidergraph A (Relaxation)

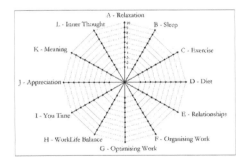

Now, let's start to use the spidergraph to reflect on whether the physical aspects of destressing, such as progressive relaxation, form a part of your current regime…

Don't forget that there is the spidergraph in the appendix at the back of this book, or you can print one off from www.teacherwellbeing.uk

I'd like you to reflect upon how much you currently destress using any of the types of techniques we have just discussed. If you use breathing exercises, or a progressive relaxation, daily, or perhaps meditate, then you may feel you should score towards the top of the scale – perhaps a 7 or 8, or even higher.

If this type of relaxation isn't something you ever do, that's down towards a 1. Mark on your spidergraph where you score – and do be honest, this is your tool for reflection and considering what changes might work for you so it's important to step back and know where you really are.

Part 4 – Stress, Well-Being and Self-Care.

Let's explore some of the most important elements of self-care. It is well established that physical and mental wellbeing go together. If you are physically rundown or unhealthy your mind isn't going to be at its best, making you more vulnerable to stresses, and if your mind is stressed it can lead to physical problems and illness.

So, to really enhance wellbeing and resilience, both mind and body need to be considered, and actions taken…

4.1 - Sleep.

It's often surprising how many people don't think enough about getting enough sleep, both in terms of its quantity and quality. Sleep is something that many take for granted, but we shouldn't…

For many reasons, getting enough good quality sleep seems to be an issue for many people in the modern world. Whether it's due to the nature of the always-on modern world with its 24/7 culture, the rise of information technology such as mobile phones and the Internet, or whether lives are generally just busier (or indeed a combination of any of these) certainly sleep is one of the aspects that can often suffer.

Statistics suggest that, in the UK, many people are not getting enough sleep. For adults, 7 to 9 hours of sleep are recommended. Is that worse amongst teachers, working late into the night to get planning and marking etc done? Well, I can't say I have the figures, but talking to teachers it certainly wouldn't surprise me...

Chronic Sleepiness is damaging...

The problems caused through having too little and/or low-quality sleep are numerous and serious. A lack of quality sleep severely impacts clear thinking and decision-making. People become less creative, and work more slowly getting less done.

New ideas are more difficult to generate and overall, our efficiency drops in a number of ways. We make far more mistakes, which can generate a number of problems. So not only are we doing less work but we are making more errors when we do so, so we may have to redo a lot of work which is both frustrating and inefficient.

Also, in terms of psychology, we get increasingly irritable when we're tired, and our mood tends to drop - let's face it, it's very hard to be excited and feel good when we're exhausted – which can also exacerbate stress.

It's not only the mental domain that a lack of sleep affects, but it can severely impact our physical well-being as well. Our immune system weakens when we are tired and with chronic sleep deprivation there's an increase in the likelihood of serious health issues such as heart problems, diabetes and so on.

One element of modern life which can seriously impact the quality and quantity of our sleep is our computer, phone or tablet screens, especially using them too late in the day. It's now well understood that particularly the blue light in a screen actually affects the sleep centres of the brain, tending to reset them to think it's daytime, thereby reducing the desire to sleep and disturbing our body's sleep clock. Even screens with a night mode which reddens the display can still have an negative effect.

However, with computers also comes the temptation to deal with emails or working too late into the night, meaning that we are still thinking of these things when we try to get to sleep – creating the problems of a 'buzzy brain'. Working on things too late at night, and with too little buffer time before sleep can mean the thoughts stay with you, leading to disturbed sleep and waking up at 3:00 AM with them still running through your mind.

However, making some important changes can really enhance your sleep, so let's look at some possibilities…

What to Do - Sleep

There are a few key things to consider when thinking about enhancing the quality and quantity of your sleep.

Firstly, and somewhat obviously, comfort. Make sure that your mattress is as good a quality that you can afford and doesn't feel like it is filled with rocks. A comfortable mattress can certainly help to achieve a good quality sleep.

Quality Sleep can make a huge difference to stress and wellbeing...

Secondly, check the light levels in the room where you are trying to sleep. It doesn't take a lot of light to disturb sleep and reduce its quality, as a light level in the room which is only equivalent to moonlight will do so. It's important to make your bedroom as dark as possible. If you have thin curtains, getting a blackout liner will help, especially if you have a lot of light outside, or in the summer season when it gets dark late and light early.

Another natural concern for sleep quality is noise which can easily disturb you. If you've got a neighbour who likes to play loud 'drum and bass' music at 3:00 AM it's a little bit of a problem, but wherever you can, keeping in your sleep space quiet can make a important difference. If noise is an issue, try using ear plugs and similar to try to block it out.

Another factor is having a regular sleep schedule. Human beings are creatures of habit, and function best with a regular sleep cycle. Having the same bedtime and rising time can make a considerable difference to your wellbeing.

Some additional elements that can make a difference to the quality of our sleep are things such as diet and exercise. We look at the overall impact of diet and exercise on stress and wellbeing elsewhere, but any people don't realise their effect on sleep.

Having caffeine, alcohol or a heavy meal that is too close to bedtime can interfere, so avoid this as much as possible, while exercise can help enhance the quality of our sleep.

Of course, a really important change that can make a powerful difference is to create and ensure that you maintain an hour buffer between using screens and going to bed. This is an obvious one, yet so many people find it hard to do. However, the positive effects of having the buffer and the enhanced sleep this can create is worth it.

If sleep is disturbed, some people fall back on chemical sleep aids such as sleeping tablets, 'Nytol', or similar. However, useful on occasions as these are, they should be used sparingly because it can create a habit of relying on them to get to sleep.

Remember that sleep is about quality as well as quantity, and I believe that they don't give the same quality of rest as natural sleep.

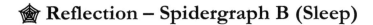 Reflection – Spidergraph B (Sleep)

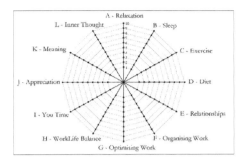

Now it's time to engage with your spidergraph once more. Score yourself in terms of your approach to ensuring you have good quality sleeping – is your room dark and quiet, do you have a comfortable mattress, is there a buffer time between screens and sleep, etc? Also, do you have a regular sleep routine?

Scoring a 10 would be that all of these are things which you do constantly, whilst a 1 is none of the above!

I would expect most people to be around a 5, with some things that they do, and some that could be improved upon.

4.2 - Exercise.

Exercise has a powerful effect on stress. Not only are you reducing the levels of your stress hormones, such as cortisol, giving an immediate stress reduction, but also it's known that high levels of exercise can release endorphins, which can elevate your mood. Indeed, the experience of the runners high where a great deal of intense exercise releases a whole flood of positive and powerful neurotransmitters is well known by hard-core exercisers.

But you don't have to be extreme in terms of the amount of exercise that you undertake, as even moderate levels of the right sort of exercise done regularly can make a powerful difference to your mindset and how you feel.

The mental focus required for some exercise can also provide a little bit of a 'break state' – that is some time away from that constant thinking about whatever may be troubling us, and can help focus and maintain psychological clarity.

Becoming fitter can also increase our feelings of self-confidence, as we look, as well as feel better. Our self-image can improve as our fitness does, improving mood and reducing stress.

What to Do - Exercise

There a belief held by many that starting an exercise routine involves a serious level of commitment such as signing up for the gym, but that is really not the case. The key is actually finding the type of exercise that works best for you, ideally one that fits well into your lifestyle. It's not necessarily about going to the gym, but exploring what suits or interests you, and what you find enjoyable. This is very individual - some people do love going to the gym, as having somewhere specific for exercise and the routine that it involves suits them. However, it also involves cost and for some people can feel a chore, making them less likely to maintain it.

However, where you may have financial challenges it's also important to remember that many forms of exercise are free and can also be fitted around, or incorporated within, other things - even walking briskly enough to break a little bit of a sweat can make quite a difference. What's more getting out away from your workspace and into nature can add greatly to the positive effects of a walk. Running, swimming, taking part in sport, or just walking more can all be effective too.

Exercise is a great de-stressor — whether at a gym, swimming, or just walking

The other important point to remember is the importance of your exercise being regular, as just doing it once a month is not likely to make a large difference. Regular exercise, perhaps daily but at least a few times a week, is crucial.

So, in terms of what to do, it's simple. Try a few things out and see what works for you!

Some Personal Thoughts

I have to be honest that I have never been really excited by exercise, especially exercise for its own sake. Even from an early age, I didn't find exercise interesting in the slightest - I was always the one who came walking back last in the school PE cross-country, etc! Perhaps unsurprisingly, therefore, going to the gym has never been for me. I wasn't particularly unfit – I walked a lot – but never really focused upon doing exercise.

However, some years ago I was encouraged to try dancing by a friend. Despite initial scepticism, I had a really good time and led to me taking it up as a regular activity. I'm not the greatest dancer, but that doesn't really matter. To me, dancing has a wonderful combination of exercise and socialising which means that it doesn't feel like exercising as such – it's just having a good time.

So, do consider the importance of finding forms of exercise that fit with your personality, interests and lifestyle. Everyone has a type of exercise that could work well for them – it's just about finding it…

⬠ Reflection – Spidergraph C (Exercise)

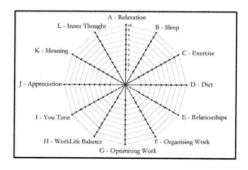

Exercise is important. How much do you do, currently? Score yourself on the spidergraph on that 0 to 10 scale, were 10 is someone that exercises to a high level most days, and 1 is a couch potato...

4.3 - Diet.

At first, diet may not seem to have much to do with stress, but its effects are far more marked than we may realise, and altering our diet can bring considerable benefits for mindset and stress levels.

It is an area of wellbeing that is very easy to ignore or to put off until you feel that you have got time to do something about it, but tackling diet now could make a surprising difference to mood, energy levels and reducing stress.

It's quick, and delicious, but sadly not so good for our health or mindset...

Research has shown that eating properly can make a large difference, not just to our physical health, but perhaps surprisingly, to our mental wellbeing also. Gut problems which can be caused by an improper diet have been found to be linked with depression and anxiety, so there is a strong link between digestive health and mental health.

One of the problems is that being under stress can cause us to eat junk food to make us feel temporarily better, and time pressure can easily turn us towards a convenient but unhealthy diet. Today, there are many convenience foods that are high in calories, but low in quality nutrition, so that with our ever pressured lives it's very easy for us to eat badly on the fly.

Changes to your diet may be worthwhile to enhance mood and reduce stress. Let's take a look at some of the easiest elements to include...

What to Do - Healthy Eating

The best general advice on diet is well known, though often ignored. You should eat good foods that are naturally healthy and fibre rich, such as wholemeal bread, fruit and vegetables. Meanwhile, cut down on fatty or fried foods, and avoid as much over-processed food as possible.

Now, with many people suffering from stomach and digestive problems such as irritable bowel syndrome, you may find it useful to discuss with a qualified professional dietitian the best diet for you as it can be very individual, and what upsets one person's digestion may be fine for another. However, generally eating healthy food and avoiding ultra-processed food will be a good start.

One of the factors that has been found to be surprisingly powerful in many studies is the constitution of the bacteria within your digestive system and its effects on mood and anxiety. For some people, taking a probiotic supplement may well make a difference particularly to digestive symptoms.

So do think about your diet. However, there are also some other everyday changes that can also help to enhance our feelings of well-being...

Hydration.

Staying hydrated can be important to how we feel. Just having a water bottle to drink from during the day is an easy starting point.

Now, many teachers have mentioned to me over the years that with the pressures in school nowadays they don't necessarily get much time for lunch or breaks or to get to the toilet, so actually drinking too much can be somewhat problematic! However, staying hydrated as much as practical can make quite a difference.

Sugar.

Sugar is an incredibly powerful element of our diet in terms of wellbeing. Recently scientists have begun to realise the effects, often sadly deleterious, of sugar within our diet. It naturally gives us energy but only for a very limited duration, meaning that we may feel energised as we get that sugar rush, but then slump, and that can actually make us feel worse overall in the long run.

Sugar may also have an negative effect on our digestive systems bacteria which, as mentioned earlier, can also directly impact our mindset.

Because of the boost that sugar gives us, it can actually seem to be addictive. Although possibly not medically addictive in the same way as alcohol and tobacco (though this is debated), it can create a habit of consumption that is hard to break.

Gradually cutting down sugar is worth exploring as an option, as this can help your mood which helps your stress levels.

Caffeine.

Often on the news we hear scare stories about the effects of drugs on people, and yet a surprisingly powerful stimulant drug is in common usage by much of the population! I'm talking here, of course, about caffeine. Caffeine is found in tea, coffee, energy drinks etc.

Are you relying on caffeine to get through the day?...

Recent research has suggested that the effects of caffeine can be surprisingly long lasting - just a few strong cups of coffee in a day can raise our blood pressure, make us jittery, and also affect our sleep, which in turn affects mood and mindset.

Now once again this is a very individual response - some people seem able to consume considerable amounts of caffeine without noticeable effects whereas others are very sensitive to it. If you find yourself drinking a lot of coffee it's worth experimenting with cutting it down to measure its effect on your feelings, sleep etc.

One other thing to point out here is that because caffeine is such a powerful drug, if you cut down too much quickly you may get side effects such as headaches etc, so reducing it gradually can be the best way.

Alcohol.

Alcohol is an obvious one. Too much alcohol is clearly bad for you, and yet when under pressure it's very easy to have that little tipple at the end of the day just to make you feel more relaxed.

As Homer Simpson once put it "To alcohol! The cause of, and solution to, all life's problems"…

One problem with alcohol, apart from obviously the long-term health challenges of too much alcohol consumption, is that although alcohol can often help you to get to sleep it doesn't help the actual quality of that sleep, and that can make quite a big difference. Too much alcohol means that you may go to sleep very easily but can wake in the early hours disturbing the desired sleep duration and quality.

Alcohol can also have some negative effects on the digestive system, so that can be problematic. So overall just keep an eye on alcohol intake, and consider whether your intake is healthy.

🕸 Reflection – Spidergraph D (Diet)

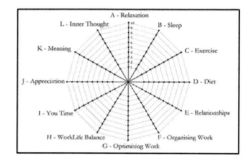

Diet can be surprisingly important, so its time to step back and consider how good is yours?

It's not about trying to be a killjoy – it can be true that a little of what you fancy does you good! However, its about balance and moderation.

Score yourself on the spidergraph on that 0 to 10 scale, where 10 is a really healthy diet, with a good balanced diet, hydration and moderation in alcohol etc, and 1 is a daily takeaway with a large bottle of wine!…

4.4 - Relationships

The importance of relationships for our mental wellbeing is well known. When we have people around us - people we can talk to, people who support us and care for us, and crucially, people we can share important things with - then we naturally feel better. So why am I mentioning relationships when it's so obvious?

The problem is twofold – time and stress. We may be so busy that we don't have time to really properly engage and spend time with the people around us. Secondly, when we are under stress, there is a psychological tendency to withdraw, perhaps we subconsciously seek somewhere quiet away from people so that we can recover. Yet hiding away and closing ourselves off from others is often the worst thing that we can do. When we are on our own, we have more time to mull things over in our mind, constantly running through those scenarios and situations which are worrying us and pulling us down.

Creating and maintaining our relationships with a range of individuals can be important in reducing stress. Not only friends and family, but colleagues and other people to talk to such as union reps and so on who can bring a new or professional viewpoint to the stresses that we face.

Perhaps most important in terms of school stresses are our colleagues, because our relationships with them can really help us to overcome the challenges that we encounter each and every day. Colleagues are likely to understand us as well as, or better, then most others, as they often have the same lived experience and pressures.

One of the challenges of high workload is that many teachers don't get the time to have those conversations that build and maintain those supportive relationships with colleagues. I know many teachers who never manage to make it to the staff room during the school day because there's just too much to do. Yet the relationships that we have at work are really important and so very much worth cultivating and developing.

Another issue is that people often don't open up to talk and share their worries and concerns for a number of reasons. For example, they may want to appear strong, and so don't want to admit challenges or problems.

Some people don't talk because they're worried about their position and feel that they may make themselves vulnerable if they admit challenges. Some may not want what they perceive to be pity from others, while others don't talk because they don't think it will help at all. Of course, some people have a very private personality, and simply want to deal with it alone.

Talking and sharing with others is important.

Yet these can make us feel more alone and increase vulnerability to stress, so don't put off having conversations and talking about issues.

What to Do – Relationships

The solutions here are obvious. Yet often you may not do them due to workload, time challenges, or simply exhaustion. However, to help you destress, it can be important to ensure that you have people around you and that you talk to them.

Also, do remember to ensure you build and maintain your relationships with those closest to you – your partner, children and close friends. It's easy to be so focused on work that we start to ignore and slowly distance from those who should be closest. Over time relationships can suffer. Make sure that this doesn't happen to you.

To enhance our relationships with colleagues, it can be really useful to arrange social events within schools where people can share and just enjoy being together. Because of the time constraints some schools have to find creative ways to build that social atmosphere – for example one school I worked with had regular early morning breakfast get togethers before school, because doing anything after school after school just wasn't practical, and it worked well for them.

There's no one pattern for the right way to do it, but do try to find what works for you and your colleagues and your school and your workload situation.

Personal Thoughts...

Now when I go into schools it's amazing how quickly you pick up the vibe of both the quality of relationships between colleagues, and staff morale. The two are usually linked – in my experience those schools which find ways to build good relationships are also schools where the overall stress levels tend to be much lower. It's really important to ensure that colleague relationships are developed, as well as partner, friends and family.

☐

⬟ Reflection – Spidergraph E (Relationships)

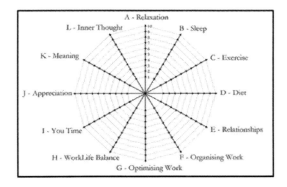

Now, consider how well you build and maintain relation ships with those around you, and score yourself on the spidergraph.

Are you currently you give those relationships the time and quality they deserve? If you are, then you may score an 8 or higher. If, however, you are putting off meeting up with friends or spending time with your partner or children, then that scores much lower!

Remember, scoring is not about intention, its about what you are actually doing right now!

Part 5 - Workload.

I don't think that many teachers would say that they are underworked! For most, workload is extremely high, and overall it doesn't show many signs of abating to a sensible level. High workload causes stress, which means that dealing with your workload effectively is an important part of reducing stress levels and staying resilient, as well as being a more effective teacher.

Background

Naturally every teachers individual situation, and so their workload, is going to different, but it is useful to explore some general ideas and principles about dealing with workload.

Workload is a huge issue for teachers...

Workload is one of those aspects where that perfectionist element of teachers personality that we mentioned earlier can cause challenges. Because teachers are driven to try to do a perfect job, they want to make sure everything is just right, and that means that they will tend to try to continue working until everything is complete and to a perfect standard.

The problem here is, of course, that everything can't be done, let alone being done perfectly. A teacher could work 24 hours a day, seven days a week, for 365 days a year and still would have more work that they could do...

So, let's explore some effective strategies and mindset for dealing with workload, and ways to better define where and how to draw the line. Each of the ideas that follows is used by many teachers across the country.

5.1 – Organising Work

In every discussion about time management, the classic 'To Do' list is usually mentioned somewhere. They are the foundation of many approaches to staying on top of workload and, simple as they are, using a to-do list does have a number of advantages. They can help to organise and prioritise work, and they reduce cognitive load because you don't have to keep in your memory what you need to do as it's already down on paper.

Perhaps one of the most surprising, but powerful, benefits of having a to-do list is that of crossing each task off when it's done. The psychological satisfaction of crossing something off the list when completed is such a benefit that when many finish something that wasn't on their to-do list, they add it to the list so they can cross it out again!

It makes sense - we do like to feel we are getting somewhere, and crossing items off the To-Do List helps us do that. So, if you're not someone who uses a to do list it's well worth looking into. The danger is, of course, that the To-Do List itself becomes a time-consuming piece of work, and we can actually use it as displacement activity by taking time to create a perfect list rather than necessarily doing the work itself.

Personally, I feel that list should be quite rough and ready and just an aid to memory and organising work rather than an incredibly detailed plan. The more time you spend creating the list, the less time you have to do the work.

What to Do - Organising and the To-Do list.

An approach that I've always found works well (and one that I use myself) is to have a ring bound exercise book for your To-Do lists. An A5 size book works excellently. On the right-hand page each day (or whatever period of time you're making the to-do list for), you write out your list, while gently prioritising the tasks to sort out which to do first. Don't spend too long on this.

As you complete each task cross it off the list with that inner feeling of a warm and comfortable glow of satisfaction at another job completed. Next day (or when appropriate) turn over and start on the next right-hand page.

Now you may wonder why we are just using the right-hand pages for the list, and what are we doing with the blank left hand pages? Well, the left-hand pages are useful, because here we jot down anything that we need to remember, using it as a notepad. So, if someone rings you to organise something and you need to quickly write down a note about it, then jot it down on the left hand page. You can put down names, telephone numbers or anything else which you might need to remember later.

This means that when you want to refer back to these things and need to find them, they are there in the to-do book somewhere. That's far better than writing things on loose scraps of paper, as these soon disappear so we can't find them when we need them, leading to frustration and a waste of time as we desperately search for them. Keeping it in one book like this can be really useful.

The other advantage of a book is that we are creating an ongoing record of what we've managed to complete each day, so we can always look back to earlier pages in the book and see just how much we've managed to achieve. Again, this can be quite satisfying in terms of giving us that sense of progress.

5.2 – Effective Prioritising of Work

Once again, in any text you read on time management, efficiency, and so on, you will come across the idea of work prioritisation. This is usually suggested to consider two factors – the importance of a piece of work, and its urgency. These two factors allow us to create a four quadrant matrix something like this…

Within each quadrant there is a descriptor of how to approach those pieces of work that fall into it, and in many ways this makes sense. Those things which are both important and urgent should naturally be at the top of our to-do list and basically done now. Low importance but high urgency tasks could be delegated, and so on.

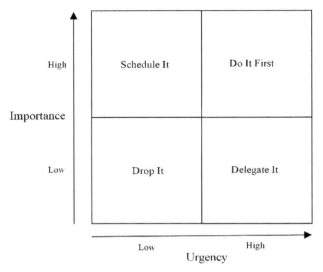

The Importance/Urgency Matrix

Given that, as a teacher you have a high workload, it's very difficult to say that you ever be able to complete all your work. Perhaps, therefore, we need to reconsider the classic importance and urgency matrix…

What to Do – Effective Prioritising of Work

What I would suggest here is to think about the urgency and the importance of your tasks but then, (and this is the crucial difference to classic time management) <u>anything</u> which is not important should be considered for dropping entirely. Let's face it, you've got so much to do so why are you doing anything that isn't important, and why would you delegate it to others who may well be as busy as you are?

This is where the perfectionism within the personality of many teachers can make them feel guilty about dropping tasks, but it is far better to spend your time on important things than waste that valuable resource on the unimportant.

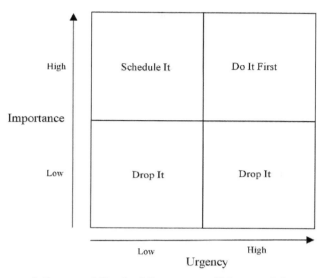

A Suggested Revised Importance/Urgency Matrix

Now obviously there are aspects here which one needs to consider in applying this, and I'm perhaps deliberately over-emphasising to encourage you to consider things differently. For instance, senior leaders in school may have a different idea of what's important than you have, and this needs to be taken into account - if SLT says something needs to be done, then it probably has to be! However, it's always worth discussing with them whether there are more efficient uses of your time.

Many teachers find it difficult to decide what really is important, so stepping back and reconsidering this can be valuable. Perhaps one useful starting point to define importance is to consider whether it is something that actually will make a noticeable difference to your pupils, your teaching practice, and/or the school. If, at the end of the day, a task or piece of work is going to have no impact on your development as a teacher, pupil outcomes, development or wellbeing, or the wellbeing of the school then it's probably not important...

Yes, at first, dropping tasks can lead to a feeling of guilt but it can make a huge difference to your workload and stress levels, and it also means that you have more time to spend on those other things that will make a difference for your pupils.

One final aspect to think about are tasks you may have to do and why they are being done in the first place. Are there things that you do on a regular basis (perhaps data collection, having meetings etc) that are only being done because they always have been done, rather than anything useful coming out of them?

So, whatever you're doing make sure you understand why you're doing it and if you're not sure, then check - it might be a redundant task which you (and perhaps others) everyone can drop saving everyone a bit of time.

5.3 – Planning Out Time

This is an obvious one, but planning out how much time you're going to spend on each task and keeping to it can make quite a difference. If you don't plan and time-limit tasks, then they become open ended, and you can spend far too much time on them.

What to Do - Planning Out Time.

"Work expands so as to fill the time available for its completion."

As part of creating your to-do list, mentioned earlier, you can also allocate the amount of time you plan to spend on each item. This helps to stop you spending too long on one thing, only to find this means you have too little time for other things that also need to be done.

Staying focused to maximise efficiency and get as much done as possible can also be important One way to achieve this is the **pomodoro technique**.

We all know that when we start a task we tend to be focused and work progresses quickly. However, after a while we begin to tire, our focus goes, and our productivity drops. Therefore, limiting the time spent on a task to only as long as that in which we remain productive can be useful. This is basis of the pomodoro technique…

Pomodoro timer in action…

This involves the setting of a timer to give a short and limited timeframe, and during this period staying focused and productive. It's called the pomodoro technique because of the tomato shaped kitchen timers originally used - pomodoro being Italian for tomato – but, of course, any timer can work!.

This is set for a period of time, during which you focus and work on that task until the timer goes, and then you stop. The time suggested is normally 25 minutes, after which you have a 5 minute break before resetting the timer and starting again. 25 minutes, for many people, is a good period to maximise productivity – after 25 minutes this starts to drop off and we lose focus, although some people prefer longer – find out what is best for you.

After your 5 minute break, you may then continue with the original task, or start a new one.

5.4 – E-mail

We know that there's not enough hours in the day, and time can seem to easily disappear. One of the greatest time sinks for many people today is e-mail. How much time do you spend dealing with emails, and is it really time well spent?

Once again technology is both a benefit and a problem. It allows us to communicate easily, but that's also the problem, as we can be flooded by emails which can take up a huge amount of our time.

There was some interesting work undertaken by Jocelyn Glei. She looked at two different ways that people dealt with their e-mails, people that she called 'batchers' or 'nibblers'. These are pretty self explanatory titles - nibblers were people who kept going back to their e-mail throughout the day, dealing with it piecemeal, whilst batchers were those who had set times to deal with their e-mail in a larger chunks. I think I don't need to tell you which was the most effective - batchers were far ahead in the productivity stakes. So, for efficiency, it's worth being a batcher, not a nibbler.

What to Do – E-mail

The most obvious, and possibly the most powerful, is simply not to check your e-mail all the time. It's very easy to get distracted when a new email comes in, especially if that little notification window pops up, but this can distract us from other important work. Instead, where possible, have set times of the day where you deal with your e-mail, and keep it closed the rest of the time. Be aware that there is often a fear in the back of our minds that if we do this that we're going to miss out on something important, but to be honest that's not likely and the cost to our productivity isn't worth it.

When it comes to dealing with emails efficiently, one approach often suggested is the 4D approach. These 4 D's being delete, do, delegate, or defer.

So, for 'delete', if an e-mail can be deleted straight away, then just do it. It's not worth keeping it cluttering up your inbox.

'Do' means that if it can be completed quickly or its high priority then do it. What is often quoted here is the two-minute rule - if it will take less than two minutes to deal with it then do so, because it saves time compared with coming back to it later.

If you need to return to it, you must re-read it and get back up to speed which is inefficient.

Thirdly, 'delegate' - decide whether the e-mail is better dealt with by someone else, and if so just send it on and get rid of it.

Finally, we have 'defer', as there are some emails that do require more detailed work and attention and those may need to be focused on another time.

The idea is to try to keep your inbox as clear as possible and ideally don't use it as a filing cabinet.

Deal with email efficiently…

If email is an issue – and it often is – try to ensure that there are organisational guidelines from your school about email etiquette. These could include important principles such as when emails should be sent – for instance they shouldn't be sent perhaps over the weekends or at in the evening due to the tendency for the recipient to try and deal with them straight away (particularly if you have got a nibbler on the other end), leading to work-life balance issues and stress.

Secondly have policies about facilities such as all-staff e-mail. For example, one school stopped most staff being able to send all-staff emails, with that privilege being reserved to a few such as senior leaders who used it very sparingly. It made a difference. Remember that when an all-staff e-mail is sent it is generating a huge amount of workload across the institution and most of the people receiving it will probably find that it isn't necessarily relevant to them. So, if you're sending an e-mail target it, and think of other people's workloads as well.

Remember your work-life balance - do you really need to check your school emails through the weekend? Is it really going to make a difference at the end of the day? If you're feeling guilty, meaning that you have to constantly check your school emails, then you are not getting the break you need. Do try to create clear e-mail boundaries.

Some Personal Thoughts

I've always been interested in ways to keep emails under control, as they can be a real problem. Personally, I find being a batcher does work well. I've looked at a few systems, but simplicity is probably best when it comes to staying on top of email.

By the way don't get sidetracked by wonderful sounding approaches such as 'inbox zero' which was developed by Merlin Mann. He suggested that every time you opened your inbox you should clear it. Now that's quite a nice idea in theory. However, after a while Merlin himself realised it wasn't actually working, as he was becoming more obsessed with clearing his in e-mail inbox than anything else. Thus, the strategy ended up actually being quite counterproductive...

✪ Reflection – Spidergraph F (Organising Work)

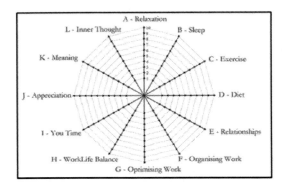

This aspect of the spidergraph is about how you organise your work – that is do you organise, prioritise and plan your time? Do you have a to-do list? Do you avoid tasks which are not important? Do you keep on top of your email, etc?

One again, give yourself a score out of 10 on the spidergraph for how well you stay on top of these factors...

5.5 - Pareto's Law – the 80/20 Principle

Another interesting aspect of dealing with workload is to consider Pareto's Law, otherwise known as the 80/20 principle.

This is not so much a law, as an experiential rule of thumb that suggests that perhaps 80% of your successes come from 20%

of your efforts, or that 80% of your time goes into dealing with 20% of your problems, and so on.

While it is a rule of thumb, Pareto's Law does remind us that some aspects of what we're doing either have success out of proportion to the amount of time we spend on them, or alternatively, some of our challenges and problems take up an inordinate amount of our time.

This is worth considering because if we can divert more of our time and focus to those things that bring great results, or deal once and for all with the 20% of our issues that take up so much (80%?) of our time, rather than just firefighting the issue, we can be more productive and less stressed...

What to Do - Pareto's Law

So the question to ask yourself is what brings you your greatest successes, and what are your greatest challenges or time sinks?

Once you are aware of these, it's then about taking some time to reflect on the optimal ways to allow us to do more of one, and hopefully find effective methods to deal with the other - once and for all...

5.6 – Time and Quality

We mentioned earlier on that the personality of a teacher is often geared towards perfectionism. Whilst in many ways an admirable trait, striving for the very highest quality at all times can actually create challenges from the sheer amount of work that needs to be done.

A teacher's workload is, of course, often excessive because there's always more that can be done. A teacher could work 24 hours a day for 365 days a year, and still not get everything completed. Therefore there naturally has to be a trade off somewhere between the quality of work and the time spent upon it.

There's always more to be done...

There is a principle of diminishing returns when it comes to the balance between the amount of time you put into a piece of work, and the final quality of it. Take doing some lesson planning for instance. It may be that in an hour you might do a OK job of it, whilst in two hours you could do a pretty good one. Of course, in three hours it might be a little enhanced, whilst in four hours very slightly better again, whilst after five hours you're now just really fiddling around the edges. However, it's still not perfect – and it never will be...

So, is it worth spending all of those five hours on your planning? Is that the best use of your time? Would it be better to stop at two hours, or even one and have more time for other things?

What to Do - Time and Quality.

The crucial question to ask yourself is whether it is perhaps better to do three things well, rather than one thing outstandingly...

In many (even most) situations, the answer is that three good pieces of work are better than one outstanding one (there are exceptions in some situations, but we are talking generally here). A key phrase that can be applied to work is 'good enough is'. It's a powerful phrase, but it's also a worrying one for many teachers because it challenges their tendency towards perfectionism.

Some might even take it to suggest doing a slapdash job, but it's not that at all. Instead it's doing work which achieves its purpose, but not necessarily investing more time and energy into it. Remember that, taking planning as our example, every extra hour you spend on it is an hour you're not going to be doing something else, which means other aspects could suffer, and other uncompleted work may weigh on your mind. It may be affecting your work life balance where you're taking time away from the family and other important things.

I would emphasis again here that I'm not saying you should do a poor job. I do emphasise quality, but if time is a pressure, then doing enough quality to achieve your aims, but not more, could be a strategy worth considering.

After all, how many times has it happened to you that you have put hours and hours into something and at the end of the day, no one has actually noticed, and/or it hasn't actually made any real difference? What else could you have done in that time?

So do consider the principle of 'good enough is'. This approach does work. I remember talking to a head teacher about this, and she was already trying to instil this idea within her staff because she was well aware that her team were incredibly driven with high standards, meaning that they were spending too long doing too little and were in danger of burning out.

There's a lot to do and at the end of the day if you get the quality and time balance right it will make a big difference to your stress levels.

Of course, if, you get everything done well enough, and you have spare time, you can go back and tweak if you want to - but my guess is there won't actually be a lot of time to do this.

5.7 - Using A.I.

Today, teachers have a new option to help them reduce workload, and that is the use of artificial intelligence, or AI. At time of writing (December 2023), AI is starting to become more capable and useful, and can only develop further..

Many teachers will already have noticed that their pupils have discovered AI. Indeed, many pupils are already using it to reduce their own school workload, by creating their essays and other homework using online technology. That is not, perhaps, ideal for their own learning process!...

What to Do – Using A.I.

For teachers, AI can create a useful starting point for some aspects such as lesson planning. Why not try experimenting with AI for creating lesson plans etc? Although you may then tweak and develop them further from the output supplied, it can provide initial ideas or a foundation structure, and overcome a mental block!

Using AI Tools can save time, and provide a foundation to develop new teaching materials etc.

I won't say a lot more about AI here, except to encourage you to give it a go, as it is developing rapidly, and by the time you read this may well be able to do even more!...

5.8 - Multitasking.

Why, in the modern world, is there is a strong tendency for everyone to try to multitask? Perhaps it's due to the nature of workload with so much to do that we tend to feel that we need to try to do everything at once. There's also a feeling that people are expected to multitask and have several things on the go simultaneously. Not being able to juggle tasks may be seen as a sign of, if not failure, at least ineffectiveness.

But we need to challenge this tendency to multitask for a very good reason — it doesn't work! A lot of research has been done on the effectiveness of multitasking, and the studies demonstrate one clear conclusion - human beings cannot multitask. Not that we aren't very good at it, but we really cannot do it in any meaningful way at all...

No - just no!...

Actually, I should perhaps qualify that we can't multitask where two or more tasks require cognitive focus and effort - where we need to think about what we are doing. However, we may be able to dual-task where one of the tasks has been automated at least to some degree.

So, we may be able to drive and talk to a passenger in a car, or iron our clothes while listening to the radio. But the moment you need to engage your thought processes with the automated task - perhaps you become aware of a hazard in the road up ahead, or maybe a tricky bit of ironing to find your way around - then that is where multitasking goes out of the window. At that point you must stop talking to your passenger, or stop listening to the radio, because our brain is designed to really focus on only one thing at a time. So, despite popular opinion, and some people thinking that they are the exceptions to the rule, the human mind really cannot multitask...

What we are actually doing when we believe that we are multitasking is in fact, task switching. We focus on one task for a short period, then switch our focus to another task for a while, and then perhaps a third task. We actually do them serially, not simultaneously. The problem with this is that every time we switch tasks, our attention needs to change from one task to another which involves a loss of efficiency and time as we need to get up to speed with the new focus.

We also know from research that when we try and multitask our effectiveness goes down the number of mistakes we make goes up. That means that we must approach our work in a certain way that is contrary to how most people try to function today.

By the way, it might seem surprising, but this also applies to young people as well. There is a perhaps a belief that todays young people who have grown up in such an information rich, multi-channel, environment are able to multitask much better than those more senior in age. In fact, though they may believe they can multitask well, research suggests that they are actually just as bad at it as anyone else. The impact of a pupil trying to multitask - for instance perhaps doing their homework, while also scanning Facebook, and watching TikToks, and listening to music on Spotify, impacts their effectiveness and that will lower their academic achievement.

Focus for success!...

Sadly, because we can only focus on one thing at a time, when we multitask we are unaware of just how much our attention and efficiency has been impacted by this attempt to do so!

What to Do - Multitasking.

If you want to de-stress, one the keys to feeling good is to be more effective, and aware that you are getting more done. In order to do better work, and be as efficient as possible, you should focus on one thing at a time using a serial task approach. Do one thing, do it well, complete it, and get it right, and only then move on.

Now there are times when we do need to attempt to multitask where, for whatever reason, the pressures force us to do so. Now in this situation perhaps the best approach is what I call 'focus and park'. This is where you focus on one task for as long as you can, using as large a block of time as you are able to, on that task, then 'park it' by putting that task away (close the document etc). Then open and focus completely on a new task, once again for as long as possible.

Basically, it involves maximising time on each task before moving on, and so reducing the frequency the task switching. It's not ideal but it can at least help.

Some Personal Thoughts...

Naturally, when I'm running workshops on stress, resilience and workload, this often leads us to an ongoing debate about multitasking, and issues such as gender differences and multitasking. Can women can multitask better than men?... In answer to this, I would simply refer to what the research suggests, which is that is <u>no-one</u> can multitask. Whatever your gender, the answer is the same!...

At workshops, a lively debate often ensues about aspects of multitasking, and often, I'm challenged by an individual that believes that they are exception to the rule. If this is you, perhaps you may like to try the following little exercise...

Recite the lyrics to your favourite song out loud, whilst simultaneously writing down a list of all the people you saw last week.

Are you actually able to do that well, or do you actually find yourself tasks switching as you try to do so?...

5.9 – Focus and Distractions

Now we mentioned in the previous section about multitasking, today we live in an information rich environment. For example, our computers can have multiple windows open at once which can mean we are surrounded by potential distractions - it's very easy for us to get drawn away by feeling we need to check email, or worse, think that we'll just have a quick look at YouTube, and maybe watch some videos of cute kittens as a little break!

Even more dangerous, if we perhaps are researching something, we can end up down the Wikipedia rabbit hole where each reference leads us on to something else interesting, and so on and so forth until we find ourselves a long way away from where we started, and having lost lots of time and produced very little.

Solution - Focus and Distractions.

If you want to be effective and efficient (and remember, that's a great way of reducing stress) then focus and focus well. As with multitasking stay focused on your main task and ideally don't have distractions around.

That means not getting halfway through a task and then opening your e-mail just to check, and definitely avoid those cute kitten videos a little break - instead just focus! I'm not suggesting you don't have breaks, they are vital, but while you are meant to be focussing on a task, then focus upon it!

Even having music in the background can make a difference. Now, I'm aware that this is a very individual thing, but I think it is worth experimenting with working in silence. After all, why are you listening to music while you work? It's often because what you are doing may be boring, so you like to have something else 'nice' to listen do in the background.

Keep focused!

However, remember our discussion of multitasking – if you are hearing the music your attention isn't on the fully work you are doing, so that task will take longer than it needs to, and perhaps will be done less well...

It may depend on what you're doing. Certainly, if it's a routine task it's probably not going to affect you much (remember we can multitask with automated tasks without as much of a problem).

If you absolutely decide you must have music on, it may be good to have instrumental music rather than songs with lyrics, but find what works best for you. Overall, do consider getting as quiet as possible in the work environment.

🕸 Reflection – Spidergraph G (Optimising Work)

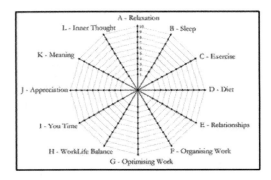

This aspect of the spidergraph is about how you optimise your work. Do you consider which elements of your work have the greatest results, or cause the largest problems as per Pareto's Law? Do you try to multitask, or do you concentrate on one task at a time? Have you tried AI? Do you adopt the idea of 'good enough, is?'

One again, give yourself a score out of 10 on the spidergraph for these factors…

Part 6 – Work-Life Balance.

6.1 – Work-Life Balance

Creating some distance by having effective barriers between work and home life can make a huge difference to your stress levels.

Earlier we looked at the personality of teachers, and the ways in which this could contribute to their being an excellent teacher. As we saw, the commitment, the optimism about people, and the rule consciousness of many all mean that most teachers want to do a great job, and go the extra mile to do so. However, this desire to go the extra mile can lead to some important work-life balance issues, which can greatly cause or exacerbate stress levels. There can be a tendency to never 'switch off', and be always working, or thinking about working.

What is needed is to maintain an positive work life balance, and that requires clear and effective boundaries. However, after years of working with teachers I have found that this is one of the key areas that most teachers put off doing anything about, probably for a few reasons…

Firstly, they feel that by creating a more positive work life balance they won't get as much schoolwork done, which challenges their perfectionism. Secondly, they can not have the urgency to do anything about work-life balance because they feel that their workload issues may be only temporary, and that they will ease very shortly. Therefore, they can survive a period where things are out of balance.

Both of these are problematic. A poor work-life balance leads to stress and exhaustion, and that leads to less efficiency. We can get more done when we are fresh and focused, and an effective work-life balance helps to achieve this.

Secondly, that release from extra pressure and workload that teachers promise themselves usually never comes. There is always something new that crops up, and so the timeframe before the anticipated relaxation and focus upon their wellbeing keeps getting extended indefinitely...

Balancing work and family life can be challenging...

One additional work-life balance challenge is that many teachers take work home with them. This means that not even home is necessarily a respite from the pressures of work, and indeed home can become just another work environment. This is certainly not ideal. So how can we deal with this, as well as the other challenges of work-life balance? Let's explore some ideas...

What to Do – Work-Life Balance

We need to create and maintain clear physical and psychological boundaries to define a difference between our personal life and our work life

One of the most effective work-life boundaries is ensuring that you do all of your work within the school environment. Despite the challenges, I know many teachers who do this, usually by getting in early and staying later, and this allows them to leave everything behind at school when they leave for the day. I am aware that many teachers say that this is impossible for them to do, for whatever reason (and it's often children and family commitments). However, if you can arrange things to leave everything behind at school, it really can make a big difference. It's certainly worth considering whether you could make that work for you.

If you are going to work at home, then it's important to create an area which is purely for work. Of course, if you're lucky enough to have a large house with a study, then that's excellent. It means that you can keep your work in the study, and when you walk out the study you're effectively walking out of work and leaving it behind. This gives the clear psychological (and physical) break between home life and work.

Most people don't have the luxury of a study, but if not, you can still consider creating a space exclusively for school work. Perhaps, space permitting, having a desk in your home that is for school work only. If that isn't possible, even just using a fold away table that goes away when you have finished can be effective. The crucial thing is to be able to separate yourself from your work environment, even if it is within your home.

We link locations with mindsets, so having a space that is associated with work, and then moving away from it (even if that is within your own home) means that psychologically you are leaving that work behind and so are more likely to be able to relax.

This is also one of the reasons why it's also really important not to do school work sitting on the sofa, in front of the television, or something similar. To explain - suppose during each weekday evening you sit on the sofa doing schoolwork, whilst watching television. Now, when Saturday comes around and you sit on the sofa to relax, what is going to happen? Because your brain now thinks of your sofa as a workspace it is going to be telling you that 'I'm sitting on the sofa, so I ought to be doing some work'. Hence, you are probably not going to be able to relax, or may begin to feel guilty that you are sitting there and not working!

Working in bed?...

This is also why taking work to bed with you is really not a good idea. Sitting up in bed doing work means that you're thinking of schoolwork last thing before you try and get some sleep - as well as staring at a bright screen (as we mentioned earlier you really need a buffer of time to wind down and to really sleep properly and effectively). You are also making work associations with your bed and bedroom just as you might with the sofa. At the end of the day, your bed should only be associated with a couple of things, and schoolwork probably not being one of them!

Finally, a tip that has been mentioned by so many teachers is to only take home as much as you are likely to be able to reasonably done. If you manage to finish that work than that's great, so why not actually have some time off...

There are other psychological boundaries you can use as well, for example having your work in a bag which you hide away when you aren't working, because if your work is out on view, you'll feel guilty if you're not doing it.

Having firm time boundaries is also really important, as work can extend to fill whatever time is available. If you're working at home, work up to whatever time you have already decided to cut off, and then finish regardless. If you work too long, you're not going to be effective, and you're going to make mistakes.

Spending time with family and friends, or getting away form work to take the dog for a walk, can recharge you, so make sure you make that time…

Teachers can also be really creative with finding ways to ensure they don't spend too long working at home. One interesting approach that a few teachers use is possibly not for everyone, but can work well if it's right for you! If you have a school laptop computer that you take home with you, why not do so, but leave the power charger behind at school?... What this means is that you have a limited amount of time to get your work done in, which really focuses the mind, and prevents your work time becoming open ended!...

Make time for other things...

Some Personal Thoughts

When talking to teachers, I have usually found that the really effective and resilient ones also have a good approach to their work life balance. They realise the importance of down time, and spending time with family and friends, and ensure that they do so.

It really is about finding what can work for you, and that means experimenting. Not every technique is right for everyone – take the laptop charger idea, for example. Some people find this a really useful technique, whilst others find it makes them actually more anxious and stressed than before! Indeed, some time ago I was having a discussion with a head teacher about boundaries and techniques, and mentioned the charger idea. He was clear that it was certainly a technique that wouldn't work for him, whereas other teachers I have talked to use it and find it really helpful! As ever, its about what works for you!...

✪ Reflection – Spidergraph H (WorkLife Balance)

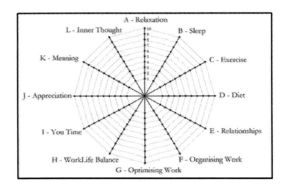

How good are you at keeping an effective work life balance? Do you manage to keep work and home life separate? Do you have a defined work area? Again, score yourself out of 10 based on your current practice...

6.2 - Switching Off

Background

An important element of controlling stress is being able to switch off, and one of the most effective ways of doing this is to spend time engaged in your own passions and interests, such as pastimes, hobbies and so on. Here, we mean something which is your own, not work related, and something you enjoy.

Now what that is, is obviously very much down to the individual. Some people enjoy doing sport or exercise, which fits nicely with another element of destressing. Other people might enjoy reading, doing jigsaws, watching sport, painting, visiting art galleries or perhaps even making a model of HMS Victory out of matchsticks!...

Finding a relaxing pastime can help reduce stress...

Whatever it is, really doesn't matter, as the important thing is to have something which gives you that break state from constantly doing, or thinking about, work. This naturally leads us to an important question - do you currently have something which you enjoy doing as a pastime? If so, do you still do it, or has school work taken over entirely?

What to Do – Pastimes

If you don't have a pastime, or if you don't have time to do the things you enjoy, then that's an indicator that perhaps it's time to do something about that.

Many teachers have hobbies and interests that they don't feel that teaching allows enough time for, but rediscovering and re-engaging with these is a good way forward. Even if you don't have a pastime currently, there will probably be something that you have wanted to try – why not do so?

We therefore need to have some way of finding the time and space to switch off from schoolwork, and do something else…

One of the ways of doing this is by using what I term a 'two-ended thinking' approach to time management. I differentiate this from the 'one-ended thinking' which is what most people do. The two 'ends' in this are work (and other commitments) forming one end, and 'you time' the other…

To explain, one-ended thinking is where you fill your time entirely from the direction of work and other commitments. So, in spending your time you start off with all those elements of work that you absolutely must do - things such as your contracted hours - the metaphorical 9 to 5. Then on top of that there are all the other aspects of work which you've really do need to do, even though it may not be part of your contracted role. Then there are those extra little bits where you're going the extra mile and helping out that little bit more, and also there are some other things which you feel that probably should do. Then, on top of that, there are chores, family and so on.

Now of course when you have completed all these many tasks then naturally whatever is left is your time to relax. This is nice but, of course, as you're aware leftover time to relax doesn't happen – you have filled your day (week, month, year...) with work and other peoples demands...

My suggestion is to experiment with two ended thinking.

In two-ended thinking you start off planning out those things that we absolutely must do. Then you add in other things that are genuinely really important plus, of course, those most important family commitments. But now, instead of now adding those extra things you feel you ought to do, you think about allocating time from the 'you' direction...

Diarise your free time, to ensure you get it...

So, starting from the 'other end' of your time (you time), book in that time for you - for those hobbies or doing those things which you enjoy that will give you the break you need. Then, whatever time is left you can fill in if you wish to do so, with more work etc. Write this in your diary, keeping that you-time as an integral part of your planning.

By consciously making the time to relax or break from work it ensures you get it. If you wait until you've finished everything that you need to do, that's never going to happen. Remember that by creating that time to relax you will be more effective, so the time will be made-up in getting things done more efficiently.

🕸 Reflection – Spidergraph I (You Time)

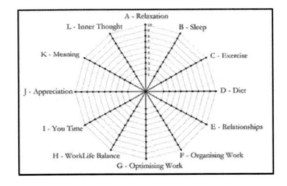

Here, you can score yourself out of 10 based on how much time you have for you. That means, purely for you – not doing things for other people!

Part 7 - Positive Psychology.

It seems obvious that we can't feel healthy, positive and happy, and also be stressed and unhappy at the same time. So, wouldn't it be great to feel good, and reduce our stress thereby? To help us to achieve this, can we unlock a few of the secrets of happiness and psychological wellbeing?

Perhaps a good place to start is the fascinating area of positive psychology, which gives us plenty of ideas for building inner resilience and well-being.

The field of positive psychology was really kickstarted with a 1998 speech given by Martin Seligman, the newly elected president of the American Psychological Association. Seligman noted that much of psychology had been focused around psychological illness. Instead, he felt that it would be valuable to focus instead on what made people feel positive and actualised, and made life fulfilling.

When it comes to happiness and well-being there's always a potential debate about nature versus nurture. Some would say that some individuals are born optimistic and positive, while others are more negative and pessimistic, and that very little can be done about it.

Now, whilst research does suggest that there is a genetic component to our underlying feelings of positivity or otherwise, this inbuilt tendency appears to only be somewhere around about 50%.

Our current circumstances in life - what is happening to us generally at that time - is about another 10% of our positivity and optimism levels. That means that 40% is pretty much changeable. That's not a small amount, and can make a significant difference to our life, let alone our stress levels! It's an exciting thought that when it comes to feeling good a lot of it is possibly within our control, provided we focus and deal with it effectively.

You can do something about feeling good!...

So, let's take a look at some of Seligman's findings that we might apply, as well as the ideas of other researchers who have made contributions which might be useful to overcoming stress for teachers, and see how we can apply these for our own well-being.

Seligman developed a 5 factor model which has the acronym 'PERMA'. The five elements are Positive emotion, Engagement, Relationships, Meaning and accomplishments or achievements. We have already considered relationships earlier, so now let's explore each of the others in turn.

7.1 – Positive Emotion

Positive emotion makes us feel good. Now this might seem a bit of a truism and somewhat recursive, as it suggests that happiness leads to happiness! So, is this useful? Actually it is, as it's not as simple as it first may seem – happiness per se isn't actually the key…

When Seligman researched various emotions, he found those which appeared to have the greatest effect on our feeling of well-being. When I'm running groups, I often ask the participants what they think these are and usually I get an interesting range of answers, usually including 'love' and 'hope'. I don't think many would disagree that love and hope are certainly important, but perhaps surprisingly, these were not the number one. Instead, his research suggested that possibly one of the most crucial emotions for wellbeing is actually gratitude - feeling appreciative about what we have and where we are right now.

Unfortunately, we have to acknowledge that most people don't do this. Instead they focus on 'if only', as in 'if only I had x, or y, then everything would be ok' . We don't appreciate all of the good things in our life right now, focusing instead on what we haven't got, or where things could be better.

There are so many amazing things around us each and every day but we just take them for granted. We don't notice them out of familiarity, or because we're too busy focusing on other more negative things. It can take something to knock us out of this way of thinking – for instance, if you've ever had a serious health scare, you will know that when you get an all clear and those existential worries you had disappear, suddenly everything seems different. Life has a vibrancy that you had missed before - you feel good, and really alive. This amazing and vibrant feeling will usually soon fade, but what if it didn't?

What if we could become really aware of the good things all around us? This could generate positive feelings which are the antithesis of stress.

Remember, the way we think is a habit. We have filters in our minds, because we are every day bombarded with huge amounts of information which we can't take in and process. So, our mind filters out the vast majority of everything that is happening around us, and thereby reduces the stream of information to manageable amounts.

These inner filters notice certain things which they have been trained to notice, or are currently on our mind. Just to give an example, let's assume that you have just booked a holiday to Spain. Now, suddenly you may notice that Spain seems to be cropping up everywhere - you might see adverts for holidays in Spain, your colleagues at work are mentioning it, and you might also notice that Spain seems to be on the TV or in the news all the time. Has Spain suddenly mysteriously actually become the centre of attention? Actually, no - you are simply now noticing it more. By booking a holiday you created a 'Spain' filter in your mind, thus you started to notice it much more. Therefore, ideally we need to create a 'good things' filter...

What to Do – Positive Emotion (PERMA)

One of the most popular and powerful techniques for connecting with sense of gratitude is writing a gratitude diary.

Each day at the end of the day write down three to five things which you're grateful for.

It is important to write them down in a journal rather than simply thinking of them in your mind, and there are two reasons for this. Firstly, writing it down makes us process things somewhat differently and more deeply, so it has more impact. Secondly, as you build up your journal, you can look back and remind yourself of just how many good things there are all around you.

Create that Gratitude Diary...

Now there's some traps to avoid when you are doing this. Firstly, it's challenging trying to find something different each and every day, and so it's very easy just to default back to writing the same things such as 'I've got a nice husband', 'I've got some great kids' etc. However, to be most effective, it's about exploring the wider range of all the things which we normally miss, or take fore granted.

Secondly, they don't have to be huge things that we are grateful for. Little things, such as just appreciating a purr when petting a cat, or some beautiful flowers in your garden, can be just as good as winning the lottery. (Well, perhaps that's putting a little bit too extreme as I think most would probably rather win the lottery, but you get the idea...). Actually, many tales abound about lottery winners and how it doesn't make them happy, so perhaps focussing on everything else could be worthwhile...

By creating a gratitude list every day, you're creating a new positive filter in your mind, and therefore subconsciously you begin to notice other positive things much more. Now it takes a while for this to happen, you won't begin your diary one night and then next day see the wonders of the universe all around you automatically, but the cumulative effect can be powerful and well worthwhile.

Personal Thoughts...

I remember running a group once and we were discussing gratitude and how we tend to take things fore granted, and I asked the participants in the audience what they were grateful for?

One of the participants said that she was grateful for hot water, which intrigued me, as it was a somewhat unusual answer, so I asked her for a little more background. She said that she'd been having building works done and so for several weeks she'd been without running hot water. Now she finally had it back again, as the plumber had reattached the pipes and the boiler was working, and all of a sudden she really appreciated hot water! I don't doubt that before long she probably would have lost that feeling of excitement again, but it was a lovely demonstration of how we can miss many of the good things a around us.

In most of the positive psychology works, the word 'gratitude' is usually used. However, I have found that sometimes people have a bit of a problem with the word 'gratitude' – for whatever reason it just feels a little wrong. Now, of course this is in many ways he said just a sign of past inner subconscious programming, but it can get in the way for many people when they try to create their own gratitude diary.

If you find that is an issue for you, perhaps use the word appreciation instead. So instead of 'I'm grateful for the flowers in my garden' you might write that you 'appreciate' the flowers in your garden in your journal. See how that works for you.

🕸 Reflection – Spidergraph J (Appreciation)

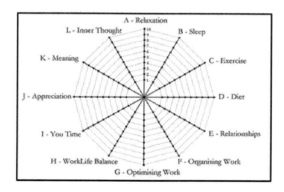

This is an important element for your wellbeing, so how much do you step back and really appreciate everything around you and in your life right now? It's easy to take this fore granted, but by appreciating what is here and now, it can make a big difference to how we feel. As ever, score yourself out of 10…

7.2 - Engagement

Background

Have you ever had a situation where you are 'in the zone', as it were - totally absorbed with what you are doing? If so, you will know that when this occurs, time flies by, and external distractions disappear. While in the zone, you just focus on whatever it is that you're doing, and it all just comes together. It can occur in different situations such as sport, in creativity, or even in our everyday work.

When Seligman talks about the term engagement, this is what he means. It is something that most of us have experienced, perhaps occasionally, or more often.

This state was studied by the psychologist Mihaly Csikszentmihalyi, who coined the term 'flow' for this experience. When we are in a state of flow the external distractions and challenges of the day disappear. If you've ever experienced this you know that when you finish whatever it is you've been engaged with, it feels great. You usually feel energised and focused. When you're in a state of flow everything just seems effortless.

Now in order to achieve a state of flow there are a number of elements that need to be in place. Firstly, the task needs to be challenging - not too easy, but not impossible either. Secondly, we've got to have immediate feedback, so that we know if what we're doing is working or not. For example, if you are playing football does that ball go in the net? Thirdly it's got to be something which is intrinsically rewarding - something which we enjoy for its own sake.

Engagement is actually one of the most challenging areas of positive psychology to apply to work but if you experience that sense of flow while teaching within the classroom, it can be really powerful. Indeed, think about your own experience. Have you had lessons or whole days where everything just worked perfectly. If so, you probably felt awesome and, crucially, in all probability any stresses would have simply melted away.

What to Do - Engagement.

Engagement, or 'flow' can be difficult to create consciously, but doing things that make you feel good and have the criteria of challenge, feedback, and reward, can make a difference. Focusing on your achievements, as we discuss shortly, can help foster a sense of mastery, and this can contribute to triggering the flow state.

7.3 - Meaning

Background

The M in Seligman's PERMA model is for meaning. 'Meaning', occurs when we are working or contributing towards something which is bigger than us, when we are doing something which we feel is important. For some people, it might be charity work, whilst for others it is scientific research, contributing to a church, or perhaps running a cub group...

Having something which is important to us, something which has an impact beyond our immediate selves, can help to contribute to a deep sense of well-being. It also makes some of the challenges and stresses of challenges such as workload worthwhile and easier to take.

At this point it's worth exploring the ideas of Amy Wrzesniewski, a psychologist and researcher from Stanford University. She undertook considerable research into the way in which people think about their work, and found that people tend to consider it in one of three ways - either as a job, a career, or as a calling.

Those people who see their work as a job see it as, in effect, transactional. They go to work to get paid, as that money helps them pay the mortgage or go on a nice holiday. It doesn't mean that particularly engaged or passionate about their work, it's just something they must do. There's nothing necessarily wrong with this but it's not always the most satisfying situation.

Other people think about their work is as a career. Here there is perhaps more interest in the work, but the individuals focus is towards advancement and moving forwards in their careers - perhaps working their way up the corporate ladder or similar.

Finally, there is the work as calling. This is where the individual is passionate about what they do. It doesn't mean that they don't want to get paid, but it does mean that they are doing something that very much aligns with their passions, values and beliefs etc. They feel that what they are doing is important.

Now think about why many people originally go into teaching. Is it simply as a job? After speaking to many teachers, I would say that it's obviously not. Although for those people with young children the alignment of holidays can be an advantage that can make teaching a more attractive proposition, most have a real passion for teaching and working with young people.

Of course, some do enter it as more of a career, wanting to work their way up the ladder. However, having met some outstanding teachers over the years of working with schools, I believe that the majority initially see teaching as a calling.

Making a difference.

As teachers gain experience in the profession, things can go one of two ways. Some teachers manage to maintain their mindset about their work as a calling, and the passion for teaching that goes with it. Sadly, others find that the pressures, stresses, and workload gradually turn it from calling into simply a job. The challenges of teaching, such as a changing curriculum, increasing problems with behaviour, challenging parents, and so on, mean that over a period of time the passion and sense of calling can be lost. From that inner passion and desire to teach and to work with young people, it becomes simply a job which has considerable pressures and not a high level of reward..

This is one of the key danger points for teachers. When a teacher loses that connection, that passion for what they're doing, the stresses begin to multiply and the pressures build up. Before long they can reach burnout, and drop out of the profession.

Therefore the key to this element of these stressing is to maintain the sense of the work as a calling, staying connected to a passion for teaching.

What to Do – Meaning

A key element of a possible solution to maintaining meaning actually occurs with Seligman's 5th element of his model – achievements – which follows. You'll find ideas for maintaining meaning there.

7.4 - Achievements or Accomplishments.

Taking time to focus upon our achievements and accomplishments can make a powerful difference to how we feel, but time pressures and circumstances may mean that we don't actually do so. Let's explore the background to this, and how you might change that approach…

Seligman's 'A' is for achievements or accomplishments. Becoming aware of these, and connecting with them positively, can make us feel good, and thereby reduce stress.

Being able to focus on what we have achieved gives us a sense of value and mastery. It also helps us realise that we are making a difference. So, this should be quite straightforward, but in practice many teachers find it very difficult to acknowledge their own achievements.

One of the reasons is that many of the improvements and wins you create for your pupils aren't immediately obvious. The results from the work that you put in to your teaching can sometimes only becomes visible years later. Therefore, it's very easy to feel that you're not making progress, and not making that difference for your pupils that you want to make. This can be demoralising.

Yet every day you do have an impact on your pupils. It may be that for the first time a pupil can spell the word cat, or understand differentiation in maths. But it's very easy for a teacher to miss these incremental steps forward, or dismiss them as they feel that that is just what they are there to do and so discount it.

But you shouldn't. By being aware those steps forward you are helping pupils to make, in whatever the level or subject, you can begin to see that you're making a difference. This, naturally, links back into that sense of meaning - working beyond on something which is bigger than you. You are helping children to develop and that's a powerful positive feeling to connect with.

You can perhaps see how this also helps you stay connected with your work as a calling - one of the reasons that teaching can slip back into being a job from being a calling is where you just don't feel that you are making a worthwhile difference. By staying focused on those wins, and really seeing your pupils development and their increasing mastery, it helps you to stay connected with teaching as a calling.

What to Do – Acknowledging Achievements and Accomplishments

Firstly, it is important to allow yourself to feel good about the steps forward your pupils are making. Give yourself permission to notice and connect with each development your pupils make – large or small. You might create a 'wins' journal where you jot down one or two good things from that day, where your pupils developed their understanding or abilities thanks to your lessons. Give yourself some time and space to celebrate those wins!

You are making a difference!

Celebrating is something that should ideally also be carried out within the school. A school which has a good vibe and high staff morale often celebrates those pupil steps forward, and enables their teachers to share them.

However, be aware that when you work at connecting and celebrating those triumphs in the classroom, you may find that you feel awkward, or that you don't deserve it. You may even feel that you aren't a good teacher. This can stem from Imposter Syndrome, and as it can come between you and developing resilience, so we'll explore that next...

🕸 Reflection – Spidergraph K (Meaning)

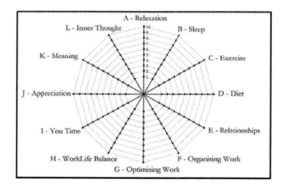

How do you feel about your job? Do you connect with the difference you are making to others? Consider the ideas in this section, and how you currently apply them to your own situation? Have you still got the joy of teaching at heart?...

7.5 – Imposter Syndrome

Imposter Syndrome is a common problem that can create uncertainty and stress. Dealing with it can not only help confidence, but thereby reduce stress levels…

Background

Not connecting with their successes is particularly marked for those people who suffer from impostor syndrome. Imposter syndrome is where, for whatever reason, people who are good at what they do and are successful just don't connect with this success or acknowledge it. Instead, they feel that they are, in effect, faking it or winging it, and constantly believe that they're not as good as people around them think they are. Because of this, they believe deep down that they are going to be found out as an impostor.

By the way, impostor syndrome is very different to what is known as Dunning-Kruger syndrome. Impostor syndrome is when you are good at what you do, but you don't connect with it, so that you undervalue your own abilities. Dunning-Kruger syndrome is the opposite, where an individual has a highly inflated idea of their own (actually quite limited) abilities. So, they think they are great when, sadly, they are not. I'm sure we've all met people to whom that applies!…

However, Dunning-Kruger is rare in teachers, whereas imposter syndrome, sadly, is not. Talking to individuals and groups about imposter syndrome does suggest that it is incredibly common. So, what are the signs to look out for?

One common sign is the fear that you won't be able to live up to the other people's expectations, and a belief that their positive opinion of you is over inflated. This may be combined with a feeling perhaps that you don't deserve success, so that when you do have successes, you disregard them and don't emotionally connect with them.

Therefore, in turn, this means that any praise or validation that you receive get rejected as being undeserved or mistaken, whereas conversely any criticism blame or failure is accepted - often catastrophically.

Now how much does this reflect you and your feelings? I would guess that perhaps these ideas may resonate quite deeply with you. If so, you are not alone. But you can do something about it...

What to Do – Imposter Syndrome

So, what are some of the ways to begin to overcome imposter syndrome?

Firstly, one of the most powerful ways is actually talking about it to others. If we stay silent, we can feel that we are alone in suffering from it, and what's more, our inner belief in our lack of ability is not challenged by others. They see us as successful and able, so they don't realise that we don't feel that way. By talking to others, not only will they help to validate your abilities but also you will almost certainly find out that many other people also suffer from impostor syndrome – people who you know are actually competent and effective teachers. Indeed, when you start talking, you may be surprised at just who does suffer from it!

The next effective way of challenging imposter syndrome is to understand that you may well have very high levels of perfectionism, creating an expectation of quality which is impossible to achieve. You need to lower that perfectionism bar. Again, it doesn't mean doing poor work, but it does mean that you need to acknowledge that sometimes not everything can be done absolutely perfectly. So, go easy on yourself and ease that drive for constant perfection, and the need to get everything done.

Now, as a teacher you may well be very well aware of the concept of the growth mindset, and even used it with your pupils. Growth mindset is a very useful idea, originally developed by Carol Dweck. She noted people tended to have what she described as a fixed or a growth mindset. A fixed mindset is where we think our ability at something is natural, inbuilt and unchangeable. For example, we may believe that we are naturally good at languages, or naturally bad at maths. A fixed mindset assumes that if we are bad at maths we always will be, it's just we're not a maths person, whereas we may be a languages person so will believe that we can learn languages easily.

A growth mindset on the other hand assumes that we all have an ability to enhance what we can do. We can improve, learn and grow. This is a really powerful idea, because when things go wrong, if we have a fixed it can be quite devastating to us as it apparently proves that we are not good at something, and if we can't do it, we probably never will. So, if we do badly at maths, we may think that there is no point in trying to improve.

A growth mindset works on the basis that if we're getting something wrong, or are unable to do it, then it gives us an opportunity understand where we need to learn and grow. Such a mindset is obviously less potentially devastating to us. It doesn't mean that failure or criticism in an area is comfortable for those people with a growth mindset, but it's not so impactful.

This idea is powerful for pupils but it's also powerful for you as an teacher. It's amazing how many teachers use a growth mindset with their pupils (remember teachers personality, and their very positive view of people) as they believe in their pupils ability to grow, develop and overcome their difficulties.

The problem is that teachers often seem to be brilliant at applying growth mindset to their pupils, but not to themselves. When it comes to their own abilities, they tend to have quite fixed mindsets. So to overcome that impostor syndrome a good approach can be to try to adopt a growth mindset for yourself, and acknowledge that there are areas where you're excellent, and areas where you may need to develop further, and that's OK.

Next if somebody says something nice about you, and gives you praise, then allow it in. Acknowledge it. Don't just reject any praise or validation, because that really doesn't help at all. Connect with that positive feeling and acknowledge that you've done a good job.

Connect with what you are doing well...

Now be aware of that little inner voice we all have (we discuss our inner dialogue in more depth later). It might be saying to you that you shouldn't feel good about what you have done, and that this would be boastful and undesirable. However, it's OK to know that you're a good teacher, and that you've done a good job. So do give yourself permission to feel good about what you've achieved.

And on the other hand when it comes to things going wrong and criticism it's OK not to take that totally to heart. Teachers tend to take criticism or errors as devastating, and that can be unhelpful and cause stress. Instead, develop the mindset of learning from challenges and mistakes, and give yourself that opportunity to grow and develop. It's simply an indicator of what you need to do right next time and so an opportunity to enhance your teaching.

Now to connect with your successes more powerfully you could create a success diary. Just as with the gratitude (or appreciation) diary we mentioned earlier, every day you could write down those wins and successes, the large and small steps forward your pupils have made.

Overall, do try and avoid comparing yourself against other people. One of the possible elements behind impostor syndrome is due to our seeing the surface appearance of other people but not what they're really thinking or feeling, whilst for ourselves, we do know what we are thinking and feeling. Therefore we compare how others appear with how we feel and they can be very different things. When others look at you they may see someone who's confident, and yet is that how you really feel? Others probably aren't as confident as you assume or they appear!

One other factor is that people tend to assume that whatever we know, or whatever we can do, other people can also. If we can do it, then it must be easy, so anyone can do it, which means that we tend to undervalue our own skills and abilities. What's more because we assume that other people can do everything we can do, but then we see them doing other things as well, we assume they must be better than us.

And yet of course this is not the case. Yes, they can do things that we are unable to, but then we can do things that they can't. Everyone has their own expertise, their own history, and their own experiences which have taught them various things. So be aware that you do have things that they don't know, and you can do things that they can't do.

Part 8 – Other Key Psychology.

8.1 - Dealing with Change

One of the aspects of working in a school environment is that change has, ironically, become one of the few constants. Change is unsettling. As human beings we like a sense of certainty - we like to know where we are, and what is going to happen, and when this certainty is taken away from us, we tend to spend a lot of time worrying, and fretting about possibilities. This increases our stress levels.

Our subconscious is designed to be constantly looking for solutions, and so when no solutions are apparent, it goes into a loop constantly trying to find one. Change often creates uncertainty without obvious solutions, and hence we can be stressed, constantly thinking and worrying. We can experience what I call 'buzzy brain' and a tendency to wake at 3am still thinking about an issue.

So, if dealing with change is an issue that causes us stress, how can we deal with it? Whilst there is no single magic solution, there are things that we can do to reduce the stress associated with change.

Firstly, make sure that we really understand our emotions related to change. Change can be of many forms, such as the loss of a role, a change in the way of things are done, or even losing our job through downsizing. Whatever it is, it can often be interpreted as a loss, and we tend to respond in similar ways as we do to any other serious loss.

One way of thinking about understanding this is the famous Kubler-Ross change curve, adapted from her other work. This suggests 5 stages of differing emotions, such as denial, anger, bargaining, depression and finally acceptance.

So, as an example, let's suppose that a new curriculum is coming in that will perhaps lead to a lot of work, or is one with which you are unfamiliar, and so uncomfortable.

There is likely to be an initial denial that change is necessary, or that it will happen by believing that the new proposal won't go ahead, and that things will stay as they are.

We don't like to deal with change...

Next, we may feel angry about all the work we put into the old curriculum and its scheme of work that is now being thrown out, or that we were not consulted, before the next bargaining stage sees us talking to SLT about how many of our old lesson plans we can include with the new scheme.

After that, the depression stage may involve a bout of demotivation and procrastination, as we avoid getting started on the new way of doing things, before we finally accept the new situation and get down to engaging with it.

Does this sequence sound familiar? Is it something that you have experienced? It may not apply to every situation, or everyone, as people do react differently, but the Kubler-Ross stages are a useful way to begin to understand the various emotions that we go through, and so help to mitigate the stresses of change.

What to Do – Dealing with Change

If change is being forced upon you, some, or all, of the emotions suggested by the Kubler-Ross model are likely to happen to you. You need to accept that, but also realise that they will pass. Whatever the change may be, you'll come out of the far side of it and things will settle down. Denying our emotions really isn't going to help things at all.

Now to help us deal with the change itself, there are some useful steps to take. Change may be for many reasons – a new curriculum or way of doing things, a change of SLT, the school joining a MAT etc...

Firstly, you need to make sure you really understand what the change is. Often, we can assume things, or only get half of the story and so we end up reacting to something which isn't actually what is really happening. This can be because of our denial, so we don't listen, or very often because the people communicating the change don't do so effectively. So, the first step is to clarify the actual situation, especially as when we do so, we often find that things aren't as bad as we thought!..

While we are in this time of uncertainty, which can be very unsettling, do be very aware of confirmation bias. Confirmation bias is where we seek out information that confirms our beliefs or worries and, in many cases, actively reject information which contradicts our expectations and beliefs. Try to look at things objectively and seek out as much balanced information from different sources as possible.

Next, it is important to look at what the change really means for you. A change may be occurring, and we might assume it will impact in a certain way, but will it? Just as you should check on the details of the overall change, ensuring you understand its actual impact on you (and others around you, if that is important) is key.

The next step may be to consider whether is anything you can do about it. Do you need to challenge the change, and is it worth doing so?

Now it is time to explore what is potentially useful or good about the change. Our minds tend towards noting the negatives rather than the positives, which is one of the reasons we resist change – we see the downsides rather than the upsides of it. However, change does often bring something good. So, ask yourself, are there good possibilities, and could it actually move some things in your favour? Yes, it's possible that there is nothing but it's worth exploring, as if you can begin to focus on the positives and seek a way forward then it can make a big difference to your stress levels.

Next, if change is occurring, think about what can you do to work with it? When we have a plan, a way forward that looks workable, it gives our subconscious a sense of possible resolution, a way forward, which means it tends to worry a little less. Remember that the subconscious is always looking for solutions, so if it has one in mind, it helps it to let go of the buzzy brain…

Now, to help with stress caused by change, it's important to remember that support from others can be beneficial. Having someone to talk things through, maybe someone who is affected by a similar change such as another member of the school team impacted by what's happening, can give us a chance to share our thoughts and ideas about what's going on in a way that enables us to offload to some extent.

Change may not be welcome, but you can deal with it…

However, be careful as it shouldn't just become a 'moan-fest' where you just keep complaining about what's going on, rather than looking for a way forward. At the end of the day, it's nice to get these things off your chest, and share your feelings but you don't want it to just go in a negative loop. So, discuss with your friend, colleague or perhaps your union representative, but do focus on possible ways forward instead of just complaining about what's wrong!

8.2 – Inner Dialogue

Our thought processes, the way we think, can make a profound difference to how we feel. They can increase, or reduce, our stress levels, so understanding and working with our inner thoughts and mindset can make a powerful difference to our stress levels.

Thought is a habit...

We all think. This thought process is perceived by many people in the form of an inner dialogue, an inner voice that tells us what's going on, what we are thinking or feeling, and so on.

For some people, this inner dialogue is very positive, and is reassuring, encouraging and motivating. Others have an inner dialogue which is much more negative, telling themselves that things are going to go wrong and it's a disaster...

Perhaps take a few moments now, to think about what you are telling yourself in your mind. Is your inner dialogue positive? Is it supportive and motivating, encouraging you to move forward and telling you that you can do it? Or is it perhaps quite negative and telling you that everything is going to go wrong?

Now, many people might assume that our emotions shape the content of this inner dialogue. Thus, if we are feeling positive and really motivated, then our inner dialogue would reflect this by telling us that everything is great etc… If on the other hand we were feeling down, depressed or worried, then our inner dialogue would be shaped by this by telling us what could go wrong, and that we need to worry about it. But is this really what happens? Does our inner emotional state trigger the inner dialogue, or is it perhaps the other way round?

It now appears that, in many cases rather than emotion leading the thoughts, our inner dialogue actually triggers the feelings that reflect it. So, if we're telling ourselves that there are problems ahead, that will make us worried, and depressed. Alternatively, if our inner dialogue is telling us that everything is going to work out OK, and that there's nothing to worry about, our feelings will tend follow that too. That's not to say that our emotional state and other factors don't make a difference, but there does tend to be a feedback loop – our inner dialogue is negative so we feel negative which in turn triggers more negative dialogue and so on.

This creates possibilities. If we can become aware of and change this feedback loop, then it could give us an opportunity to reduce negative feelings and stress. Now that means we need to change either our dialogue, or our emotional state, to feed back more positively. Changing dialogue is far easier than directly altering our emotional state, so that is a good place to start...

What to Do – Inner Dialogue

So, how might you change your inner dialogue to something more helpful? Here are some steps…

1. Become aware of your inner dialogue, and what it is saying to you.
2. Challenge it – negative inner dialogue can often catastrophise.
    a. Are things really as negative as they seem?
    b. Is the worry actually likely to happen?
    c. Is it the end of the World if it did?
3. Create a new, more positive and realistic dialogue.
4. Keep this going – it takes a while for a new habit of thinking to be created.

This approach does actually work for many, and can be used both for immediate impact, as well as longer term change. The way we think, our inner dialogue, is a habit and the more we use positive dialogue, the easier it becomes until it becomes an automatic habit.

Be aware of your inner dialogue...

Remember, if your inner dialogue is positive, it can make a great difference to your stress levels...

8.3 - Affirmations

Many people have used affirmations. These are simply positive phrases that are repeated often to yourself. The idea is that, through repetition, these suggestions will sink down into the subconscious to help guide thoughts. Some use them to try to draw success to them (in a 'Law of Attraction' way) , but as a scientist I'm not convinced that this is really effective!

However, they can help to maintain a positive mood, which can in turn enhance our effectiveness and success as well as reduce stresses.

There are some important elements to remember when doing affirmations. I mentioned earlier that not every technique works for everyone, and some people may react negatively. The same is true of affirmations. Research suggests that the positive phrases should be framed differently for those with high self-esteem then those with low self-esteem. The method that follows highlights these differences.

What to Do – Affirmations

Select on or more affirmations that you would like to use. These should be short and framed positively. The research suggests that for those with high self-esteem they should be framed in the present tense, whilst for low self-esteem they should be framed as future tense.

Thus, some possibilities (High self-esteem/Low self-esteem):
- "I am calm" / "I will be calm"

- "I am relaxed" / "I will be relaxed"
- "I work effectively" / "I will work effectively"
- "I focus on important work" / "I will focus upon important work"

While you think your affirmations, visualise yourself doing or achieving them. Repeat as often as possible, several times a day.

Personal Thoughts...

Some time ago I was working with the staff in a primary school, talking about inner dialogue and its effects, and one of the teachers in the group shared that, every day, as she drove to work, she consciously told herself in her mind that it was going to be a good day. It was as simple as that, she just focused on creating a positive inner dialogue and she found it made a quite difference in shaping her mindset as she approached her day.

By making a conscious positive start to the day, the day really could go better, and a good day is a lower stress day!

So, what do you say to yourself?

✦ Reflection – Spidergraph L (Inner Thought)

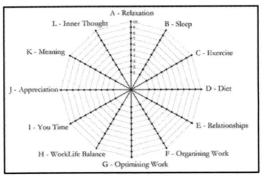

Becoming aware of our thoughts, and taking control to make them more positive and helpful can make a huge difference.

So, are you aware of your inner dialogue, and how it affects you? Do you consciously try to think more positively (perhaps by using affirmations, or similar)? Score yourself out of 10...

This is the final element of the spidergraph, and provides a great opportunity to step back and consider the changes you may make, as we discuss in the final short section...

Part 9 - The Plan

In this book we've explored a wide range of different ideas. As I mentioned at the start, think of it as a buffet of ideas and techniques, from which you can take those elements that will work most effectively for you. No teacher probably could, or would want to, do absolutely everything suggested within, but there are ideas that we have explored that I am confident will be relevant, important, and useful to you.

Change comes from within. You are the only person who can really make that difference to your resilience, and that starts with your decision to do something differently.

Resilience in the classroom makes a difference to you and your pupils...

The spidergraph that we've used is designed as an aid for you to consider where you might make those key changes. So, take a look at it now and decide what you could do differently, and then review the tips tools and techniques for those areas you feel you need to make a difference to your stress levels.

By de-stressing, giving yourself time and space to make the difference to how you feel, it can make a huge difference to you as a teacher. When you are relaxed, and resilient, you have more energy and focus. You will make less mistakes, and are able to do more in less time. It can make a positive difference to your relationships with your partner, family, or friends .

Finally, it can make a crucial difference to your health and overall well-being. Being under stress over time is physically damaging, and can lead to illness and multiple health problems.

So whether it's getting a new mattress to sleep better, adopting a whole new mindset, or adapting your approach to workload, do make that difference - decide what you want to do, and do it.

Don't forget that there are more resources, audio guides, suggestions for further reading, and more at my website www.teacherwellbeing.uk

Good luck. I'd be delighted to hear about any tips and techniques you may use yourself to reduce stress and deal with workload.

The new you starts here…

Mike Culley
December 2023

Appendix – The Spidergraph

On the next page is the spidergraph. You can fill it in in the book, or download a copy from www.teacherwellbeing.uk .

It has a number of sections, each of which specifies one aspect of resilience, stress management and/or workload. As we go through this book, we will explore each of these in turn, and I would suggest that, when prompted, you carefully rate yourself out of 10 in terms of how well you are using that approach, or dealing with that aspect of resilience.

This should be scored by reference to what you are actually doing now – not what you intend to do, or what you feel you should be doing! Also, do be honest with yourself, as its vital to get an accurate picture of areas you may need to consider developing.

By doing this, you will build up a valuable overall profile to help you to identify those areas for possible change.

That doesn't mean that other areas are not important to consider making changes in, but it should certainly give you a starting point.

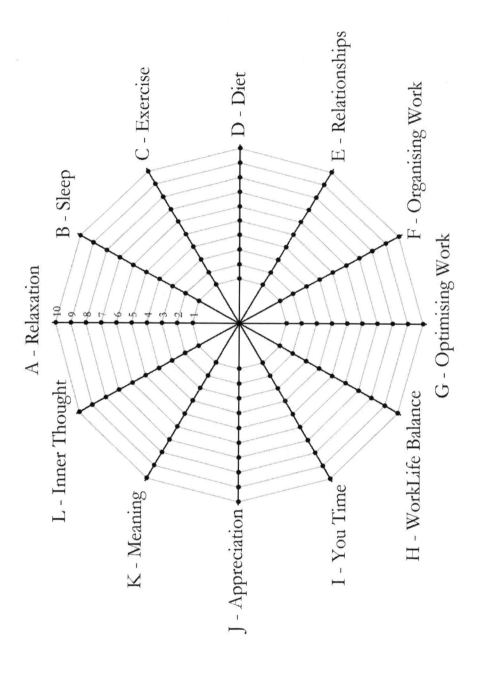

Mike Culley C.Psychol. AFBPsS

Mike Culley is a chartered occupational psychologist, with a background in enhancing individual workplace performance, and applying practical psychology solutions to real-world situations.

He has worked with teachers, schools and teaching unions for over 20 years to help educators develop resilience, deal with workload, and thrive in a challenging environment.

You can find more resources, including audio guides, suggestions for further reading, and much more at his website for teachers, at **www.teacherwellbeing.uk**

Printed in Great Britain
by Amazon

41918621R00086